Ultimate
HORSE BARNS

R A N D Y   L E F F I N G W E L L

Voyageur Press

Dedication

· ·

For my mother, Lonny Leffingwell

*Schools taught me to read and write. My mother taught me
the love of reading and the joy of writing.*

First published in 2006 by Voyageur Press, an imprint of MBI Publishing Company, 400 First Avenue North, Suite 300, Minneapolis, MN 55401 USA

MBI Publishing Company titles are also available at discounts in bulk quantity for industrial or sales-promotional use. For details write to Special Sales Manager at MBI Publishing Company, 400 First Avenue North, Suite 300, Minneapolis, MN 55401 USA.

On the Cover:
Raegan Knotts waits patiently while her horse Leroy satisfies his curiosity about activity behind him. Farm owner John Hall asked architect Tom Croce to provide him a clean interior with no exposed beams to catch dust, breed cobwebs, or attract birds. The stylish barrel vault funnels light into the interior.

Frontis:
When some friends learned Don and Karen Cohn were establishing their horse farm near Ramona, California, they gave the Cohns a pair of replica Roman-style horse head sculptures.

Title Page:
As the sun rises across Fork Farm, stables manager Samantha Berber leads two of owner Jim Cogdell's Irish sport horses up to the barn for morning feed. Barn designer Herbie Hames has described the lovely timber frame structure as "a black-tie resort for horses."

Back Cover *(top)*:
Samantha Berber walks Fork Stables' main aisle at sunrise to begin her day training and caring for the owner's Irish draft horses and Irish sport horses. The timber frame building stretches 185 feet from end to end.

Back Cover *(bottom left)*:
New York Architect William Wiesenberger designed this horse barn for New York financier James Cox Brady in 1913. Above the entry rotunda, a glass ceiling served as the floor of Brady's second-floor lounge and trophy room topped with a Tiffany skylight.

Back Cover *(bottom right)*:
In Freedom Farm's well-lit, spacious tacking stalls, Raegan Knotts, left, looks at Pete while trainer William Rodgers fits a bridle to Aequus before exercising the Arabians in the nearby indoor arena.

Leffingwell, Randy, 1948-
  Ultimate horse barns / Randy Leffingwell.
     p. cm.
  Includes index.
  ISBN-13: 978-0-7603-2441-7 (hardback)
  ISBN-10: 0-7603-2441-7 (hardback)
  1. Stables–United States. 2. Horses–Housing–United States.
  I. Title.
  NA8340.L44 2006
  728'.9220973–dc22

                                    2006015614

Editor: Amy Glaser
Designer: Brenda C. Canales

Printed in China

Contents

Introduction

Beauty, just like the concept of "ultimate," lies in the eyes of the beholder. The collection of horse barns and stables in this book constitutes one collection and one definition of the term "ultimate horse barns." Their innovation; clever response to site challenges; beauty; meticulous attention to details, equine health, and safety; or their historical context, have contributed to their selection. Some of the historical structures in this book remain in active use 100 or 125 years after their construction.

Some of these facilities exist for specific purposes. In them, their owners breed, birth, and house racing horses. Or they are homes to hunter-jumpers, dressage competitors, or working draft horses. Most of these barns, however, exist for pleasurable needs. Certainly, thoroughbred horses must work for their room and board, as do police mounted-unit animals. The horses used for carriage tours around New York's Central Park, as well as those sturdy breeds the Amish rely on for farming throughout Pennsylvania, Ohio, Michigan, and elsewhere, also work for their living. But for most of the past century, horses in North America have been bought and housed for the pleasure of their owners, and that has driven an evolution in the design of these buildings.

In the early years of this country, the quality of animal husbandry was poor. Horses, cattle, and pigs ran free in the woods, surviving as well as they could. Settlers hunted pigs and even cows as wild game, and when they could, they rounded up cattle and horses to brand them, but the animals were released again because fencing essentially did not exist. The quality of livestock diminished, and horses became smaller.

The growing wealth throughout the eighteenth century drove a desire for higher quality cattle, pigs, and horses. Wealthy landowners sought out the best horses to ride while carriage, coach, and freight wagon owners needed stronger draft animals. English and Dutch immigrants around Rhode Island crossbred horses they imported to create America's first native breed, the Narragansett Pacer. America's "Post Riders," those hearty souls providing mail service between Boston and New York, rode pacers, and legend has it that Paul Revere warned of the British invasion aboard a pacer. In Pennsylvania, German immigrants developed a docile but muscular and powerful horse in the Conestoga Valley to pull the long-distance freight wagons made there. Farther north, horse breeders in Vermont produced the drafter, another powerful animal primarily used for farming. But

New River Farm—Leesburg, Virginia
Modern building technology, whether steel beams or glue-laminated wood trusses, allow architects and riders to create and enjoy vast indoor arenas to train, exercise, and enjoy their horses year-round.

beyond these work animals, a market grew for handsome riding and carriage horses. Among the first of these was the Morgan horse, another New England native, although this handsome breed proved capable of heavy farm work.

In late August 1859, Edwin Drake sunk his first oil well and struck an economic boom. The discovery of oil in Titusville, Pennsylvania, quietly signaled the end of the workhorse era, even though oil's initial use was for lamp fuel. While engineers and chemists struggled to find processes and new uses for the smelly stuff, farmers all over the continent still devoted 20 percent of their fields

to feeding their working stock of horses. Inventors such as Henry Ford, who was born on a Michigan farm and grew up hating the "back-breaking drudgery of following a farm horse down a field," hastened the evolution to self-powered transportation and power farming. "What a waste it is," Ford once remarked, "for a human being to spend hours and days behind a slow-moving team of horses." His all-black Model T in 1908 was a motorcar for the masses, and his compact and equally affordable Fordson tractor (introduced in 1915 and available only in gray) provided equal benefit to farmers. The first years of the twentieth century saw the United States as the world's greatest producer of agricultural exports. Despite Ford, this was accomplished almost entirely with four-legged horsepower. The U.S. Department of Agriculture recorded 14,364,600 horses on farms and ranches across America in 1897, ranging in value from just $13.41 per head in Oklahoma to $75.25 per animal in Rhode Island. Prices averaged just $31.50 nationwide. Yet what Henry Ford and his competitors could not accomplish, World War I did.

The war in Europe began in August 1914. Early in 1915, the Wall Street financial firm of J. P. Morgan became the purchasing agent for the British government. Morgan's first assignment was to acquire $12 million worth of horses at roughly $100 per head. (Prices peaked for choice draft and carriage horses in 1915 at $250 per head, while the average for all horse sales reached $111.) Horses pulled supply wagons, cannons, and ambulance carriages. As fast as breeders in the United States could raise them and train the horses, the U.S. Army shipped them to England and France. They were the only thing that could pull men and materiel through mud and slop. While tanks and barbed wire began to appear toward the end of the war, horses still did most of the work and they died by the thousands on battlefields in France, Germany, and Belgium. On entering the war, the American Expeditionary Forces took 182,000 horses to Europe for their own uses. In a single year, 1917,

One of the architect's challenges is site planning and positioning the barn to take advantage of prevailing winds. This ensures the best air quality for the horses. The other consideration is locating an indoor arena so its scale doesn't dwarf the barn.

veterinary hospitals in Britain treated 120,000 horses for injuries or diseases. By the Armistice in November 1918, the United States had provided hundreds of thousands of horses, and 45,000 still were there.

After the war, the automobile completely captured the imagination of the wealthy who had taken to them as novelties a decade earlier. In 1900, there were 12 auto companies and together they manufactured 4,000 cars. By 1903, 57 companies went into business and the same year 27 went broke. In 1910, production reached 187,000 automobiles. That same year, more than 1,000 U.S. companies promised, attempted, or actually produced tractors; two-thirds of these were gone within a decade. Horses remained on small farms for decades as owners wrestled with the equation in which their work animals consumed a fifth of their profit compared to a tractor that drank gasoline that cost them money at the general store or the blacksmith shop in town. After World War I, to hasten the changeover, tractor makers began to accept horses on trade-in for their machines.

Still, the beauty of equine musculature, the pleasure of controlling a powerful animal between a rider's legs, the thrills of riding fast around a flat track race course or jumping over country fences and cantering across meadows chasing a blue ribbon or a ticking clock or an elusive fox were too seductive for those who still could afford it. In the first third of the twentieth century, horses in North America

John Blackburn, architect of New River Farm, is a devotee of natural light in barns and advocates discrete use of diffused skylight panels. His careful builders keep beautiful wood beams wrapped during construction to protect their surfaces.

(left) Dormer windows and an elevated monitor roof flood the barn interior with light and fresh air. Architect-designed barns allow owners to incorporate personal preferences and introduce design style into the function and appearance of the building.

One stall front is test-fitted. Wood panels will fill in the lower left and lower right squares, while the fully open door enhances ventilation and air quality and allows stable staff to see quickly if a horse is down.

(right) Chan-Tina Ranch— Ojai, California
A less costly solution for many barn owners, especially those in the West, is a structure such as this Barnmaster prefabricated barn. The California company will tailor its designs to meet owner's needs based on the logical grid configuration.

went from working for their living as beasts of burden to being animals that existed mostly for the pleasure of their owners, approaching the status of pets, which is where many reside today.

When horses worked for their living, the food they ate and the space they consumed in their barns was scrutinized with care and an eye toward economy. Many barns provided standing stalls only with room just to head the horse into its feed and water, but no extra luxurious accommodation for the animal to turn around or lie down. Barns were wood, and builders and farmers stored feed overhead because that was how it had been done for centuries before, and it was convenient. Trained architects designed few if any of these barns. Most were constructed by itinerant builders and crews who put up variations of what they had assembled a dozen times before. Dust filled the air in these barns, and when the flammable materials ignited, the heart-breaking tragedies extended beyond merely losing the large structure.

Even through World War II, horses worked as mounts for cavalry units, but they were no match for German tanks and machine guns. One apocryphal story, fabricated by Italian newspapers, held that a savagely horrific battle between Polish mounted cavalry and German armored units decimated the Polish Army. It never happened, but the German Army used it as devastating propaganda. By the 1940s, it was armor-plated, half-tracked trucks that pulled Allied cannons into place, and horses saw less and less combat, relegated to duty

This three-stall prefabricated raised center aisle barn offers an enclosed tack and equipment room and a double stall-size storage area for feed and bedding storage. The monitor-type elevated central roof aids ventilation.

(right) Churchill Downs— Louisville, Kentucky
One of the world's most famous horseracing facilities boasts 48 nearly identical horse barns (although there is no barn number 13). This is one of two receiving barns for horses in for one race the day they arrive. Bedding, hay, and manure are recycled into compost, some of which is chopped for fish food.

far behind the lines tugging wagons between supply depots. By the end of the war, the U.S. Army had converted its cavalry from mounted equestrian units to mechanized groups. Major sources of horses, such as the Government Morgan Horse Farm at Weybridge, Vermont, lost contracts to provide animals to the government. Washington deeded the elegant old Victorian barn to the University of Vermont in Middlebury. UVM continues its breeding and training activities for private recreational riders for pleasure and competition.

The evolution from mounted equestrian cavalry to trucks and tanks altered the composition of America's competitive teams in international horse riding events. The U.S. equestrian team members historically had come from U.S. Army Cavalry officers' corps. The end of federal funding opened teams for women to join, and the U.S. Equestrian Team, headquartered at Hamilton Farm in Gladstone, New Jersey, soon had as many successful women riders as men. Two of them, Carol Durand and Norma Matthews, won an event at the National Horse Show in 1950.

The passion for horses that drove farmers to care for and feed the animals that helped their farms work had, if anything, deepened in the last half of the twentieth century. Increasing leisure time and an expanding economy have allowed private individuals to own, board, and ride horses at commercial stables or in barns on their own property. That passion has

encouraged ongoing concern for the horses' well-being, their health and safety, and for the health and safety of those humans who work around them. In addition, attention to matters of air quality and reducing as much as possible any risk of disastrous fire now rank foremost among the issues architects consider when they accept commissions for new horse barn designs. Contemporary building materials limit those risks, while also making routine maintenance easier and less costly.

The owners who consented to be in this book are deeply passionate about the horses in their lives. Start a conversation with John Hall at Freedom Farm Equestrian Research Center in Ravenna, Ohio; or Olympic gold-medal-winner Joe Fargis at Stoneleigh Farm in Middleburg, Virginia; or Don Cohn at Ballena Vista Farms in Ramona, California, if you doubt this. The weight of their words and the emotion in their voices make their passion clear to listeners.

There are three ways a horse owner can find a barn. There are prefabricated structures available from companies such as Castlebrook on the West Coast, Morton Buildings throughout the Midwest and East, Barnmaster, and others. These offer very competent products that make some accommodation to regional differences in weather, air

Churchill Downs' horse barns are behind the track's backstretch. Ultralight racing saddles await the afternoon events, while in the background the track's signature twin towers cap the classic grandstands.

(left) Tony Terry, Churchill Downs' director of publicity, characterizes the track's barns as "the Great Equalizer." All stalls are 10x10 feet and the difference between yesterday's Kentucky Derby contender and today's winner is the extra foot or two of bedding material that grooms will provide for the winner. Leg wraps and saddle blankets hang to dry.

quality, and stabling practices. These are the most affordable. The next most affordable way to find a barn is what is called design-build, constructed to order by builders with enough experience putting up barns that they feel confident doing the planning as well. Because many of these contractors are regional, they may have a feel for local climate, practices, and riders. These structures offer a more personalized approach than the prefabricated barns, and they cost more. The final approach is to hire an architect. Each of the architects whose work appears in this book is passionate. For them, two goals work to mutual advantage for their clients: equine health and safety can fit naturally in an attractive building that is cost- and labor-efficient. Barn owners, riders, and stable hands each spend hours in these buildings. These perceptive and creative architects recognize the human-animal intersections, and readers and viewers who follow the text and look at the photos will recognize areas where social interaction takes place. Here, horses are bathed, groomed, or tacked up in a place that feels comfortable and safe for them and inviting for their owners and riders. People linger in these places, and relaxed, secure horses rest easily. The passion these owners have for their horses has manifested itself in great architecture, whether it was Sir Henry Pellatt in Toronto at the turn of the twentieth century or Ros Smythe in Massachusetts at the turn of the twenty-first century. It is the recognition of how this complex interplay occurs between horses and humans that makes each of these barns an ultimate horse barn.

This style of barn is known as a Belmont because stalls fill the center of the barn and an enclosed track surrounds the stalls so grooms can walk the horses on inclement days. Each barn contains 15 to 20 simple box stalls.

Freedom Farm Equestrian Research Center
Ravenna, Ohio

The Ultimate in Research Farms

"I always liked horses but I never had any intention to be around them. I grew up in a little village in England after the War." John Hall explained his interrupted infatuation with horses as he walked down the center aisle of his barn in eastern Ohio. "My grandfather was the village baker and he delivered the bread with a horse and cart. The milkman was the local farmer and he came around with the horse and cart. Once I entered a business career, I didn't think I'd see a horse again!" Then he laughed.

Fate exercised its own options. As Hall planned the sale of a successful entrepreneurial venture, the Diaper Genie, in he summer of 1998, a local charity horse show approached him for partial sponsorship. "We had investors and we couldn't spend money like that," he explained. A few weeks later, Mary Thomas called him again and said, "If you can't sponsor the show, how about a class?"

"Can we do something that would involve ladies and babies?"

"Ladies class," she replied. "Ladies sidesaddle."

"How much do you want," he asked.

"Fifty bucks," she told him.

"Little did I know Mary was the vice president of the World's Sidesaddle Federation, Inc. We got talking and one thing led to another. I agreed to help sort out their federation, to help promote it for just a little while, just a year, while I was looking for my next venture About a year later, I saw a horse at a local show and thought I could kill two birds with one stone by sponsoring WSFI for a year while the horse wore my company logo on its saddlepad. The horse was owned by Frances Patterson." Hall smiled at the life-changing commitment. Patterson was a great trainer of horse people, teaching them about themselves and about their love of horses. In Hall,

First sunlight reaches the formal façade of John Hall's Arabian horse farm in eastern Ohio. Designed by Tom Croce, the building is highly functional and very elegant.

Heavily insulated French doors sit open in the morning sunlight. Inside them, Dutch doors bring in ample fresh air in warmer months, while allowing horses to watch the world outside the barn.

she found an unexpectedly keen student who hung around long after the first year.

Hall characterizes himself as a detail man and a meticulous planner. To reach the success he achieved in business he had to be. He entered the world of ladies sidesaddle with his typical audacious drive. Frances and his wife wanted to honor equestrian history, and they found a picture of Empress Elisabeth of Austria, a famous horsewoman who was involved in the development of the "leaping head" in the sidesaddle.

Sidesaddle configuration led Hall to England's Barry Swain, who also was working on redesigning conventional astride saddles. Swain had just developed and patented a new design. To Hall, this was a business he could comprehend and one that interested him as someone who had marketed products to women from 15 to 50 for his entire career.

The traditional English sidesaddle has two pommels. The top one supports the rider's right leg. The lower one, known as the leaping head, is a kind of emergency brace for the rider's left thigh should she find herself off balance or unseated during a jump. Even quick maneuvers during an exhibition drill make the leaping head useful for riders.

Empress Elisabeth rode in fox hunts in England and Ireland between 1876 and 1882, and the lower pommel allowed her to lock her leg into the saddle for the jumps. She was as celebrated for her riding skill and courage as for her elegant riding costumes

Two of John Hall's Arabians enjoy the afternoon sun. "We wanted them to be able to look out, to see other horses," he said, "or what is going on inside the aisle or outside the stable. They all can hang their heads out and see what is going on."

and hats. Hall and his wife went to a tailor on London's Saville Row to have a costume and hat made for their young rider, Raegan Knotts. Hall initially wanted to work with quarter horses as the largest breed group, but switched to Arabians. He bought Miss Olive, "The Big O," and 6 months later she and Raegan won their first national championship.

"Horses demanded a complete team; I am a businessman, not a horseman," he expalined. Hall found an equally dedicated trainer, William Rodgers, and with a growing collection of horses, a show rider, and a trainer, he needed a barn and training arena, especially when Bill brought Aequus, the most successful park horse in the history of the breed. As he scoured Ohio for architectural inspiration, he found Tom Croce, whose office was in Lebanon, a four-hour drive from where Hall had found property he liked.

On the property there was a tired metal-sided pole barn with a wood-trussed roof. It had potential, Hall thought, and he and

Rodgers first talked with Croce about an extensive remodel that would add offices and an attached arena. But Hall was restive and agitated. One day over lunch he asked Croce if he could get a new barn for the money he had committed for the remodel.

"He was miserable," Croce recalled. "I came to learn that he was so unhappy with the cost of the project versus what he was getting for it. But would he be happy with a new one for the same amount?" It was a businessman's calculation of return on investment. Hall decided to start from scratch. "His expectations were never unreasonable, but he never settled for less than your best. Over the next two-and-a-half years, he made people tear things out and do them over, a bit more often than most contractors like," Croce added.

"What inspired him was a pretty nice six-horse barn that we visited to see the stalls they used. He liked what he saw there. He didn't tell me anything specific about how his new barn would look. I just took away the character of the place, an

Raegan Knotts waits patiently while her horse Leroy satisfies his curiosity about activity behind him. Farm owner John Hall asked architect Tom Croce to provide him a clean interior with no exposed beams to catch dust, breed cobwebs, or attract birds. The stylish barrel vault funnels light into the interior.

At the northern end of the barn, Croce designed an office complex that visitors glimpse as they reach the property and see more clearly from the grassy alley that horses and staff use to get the animals to their turnouts. The tall barn and office complex rooflines hide the large indoor arena behind the barn.

image. It had an air of quality about it, an air of elegance. John has a certain pride in his accomplishments and this place fits his character." Hall also had fallen in love with his horses.

Like many successful business leaders, Hall did exceptional research but he kept an open mind toward new information or new ideas. Croce learned quickly that presenting his client with enough data for him to make fully informed decisions deepened the trust between them. For Hall, everything boiled down to a large handful of concerns. He was making a serious investment in Arabian horses and he wanted them healthy and safe. But as he worked with Rodgers and Croce, who is a rider, Hall learned that more was required. A comfortable, secure horse, Rodgers convinced him, will learn better than one that is anxious or stressed.

"We know today that so much success in human athleticism is down to diet and nutrition," Hall explained, "to the sports

physiologist and psychologist, never mind the training. The goal is to make sure that your player is fit, healthy, and mentally ready to play on the day of the competition.

"Take that same philosophy to the horse. They're mammals, just like us. Their smaller brain just places a greater responsibility on the owner and trainer to create a good environment because they still have the same emotions.

"Because a horse is a prey animal, it looks sideways, it wants a lot of room around it. We wanted them to be able to look out, to see other horses, or what is going on inside the aisle or outside the stable. They all can hang their heads out and see what is going on."

"I firmly believe," Tom Croce explained, "that any time you bring a horse into a barn, they are subjected to some level of stress. We tend to focus on stall size, 12 by 12, 14 by 14, or

John Hall adjusts the halter on Leroy before grooming. The barn has two large, brightly lit tack-up stalls near the front door and adjacent to the large indoor arena.

(below) Trainer William Rodgers felt strongly that the walls between horses should be made solid so that each animal would have privacy while eating. With the arched stall front hardware and Dutch doors along the outside walls, the horses have plenty of opportunity for socializing.

10 by 10. But as long as a horse can move around comfortably it doesn't matter because there's more to it. If their stall is 14 by 14 but it has solid walls, a solid door, and low ceilings, the horse is going to be nervous. If they're in an open, airy space where they don't feel confined, that can have an impact on how destructive they are to the barn. Of course every horse is different and they deal with stress differently. But head bobbing, weaving, cribbing? There have been studies that show this is stress-related, so creating an environment for the horses that decreases the stress is worthwhile."

A worry to every horse owner and barn designer is fire. There's no such thing as a fireproof design, but there are ways to minimize the danger. There also are ways to reduce the risk of lost lives. Doors to the outside aid ventilation on warmer days and allow stable hands to remove horses quickly and safely without walking them up a center aisle. No one needs to run into the fire to save the animals. One of Hall's next concerns became Croce's biggest challenge and greatest accomplishment. Hall insisted on heating the barn and its attached 100x200-foot arena.

"We have a thermostatically controlled system here," he explained. "We let it go down to 35 degrees overnight. We don't want it to freeze but we let the horses get cold. It goes up to 45 in the daytime and we have it at 50 in the arena. There are no big temperature jumps in here and we allow this place to operate as

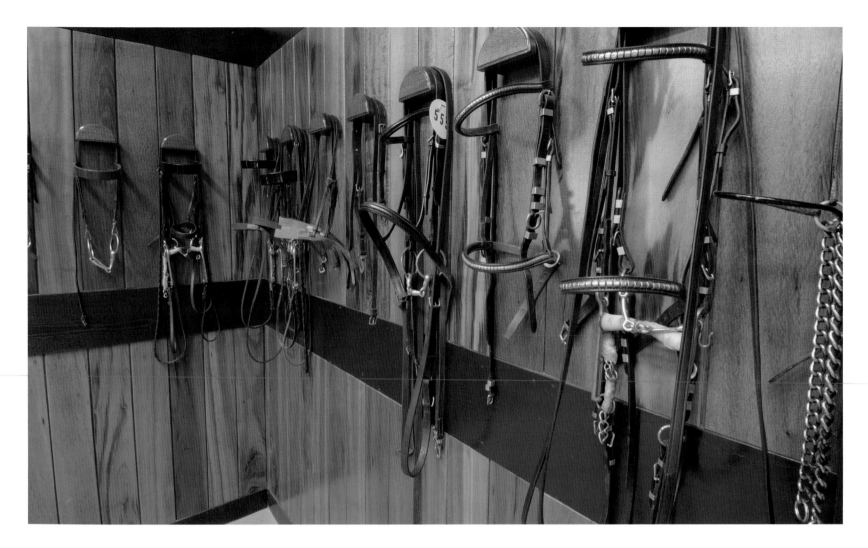

(above) A corner of the large tack room is devoted to an assortment of bridles and bits. Saddles line an opposite wall while a large granite-topped center island provides plenty of work surfaces for tack adjustment and cleaning.

(right) One consideration Rodgers (right) and owner John Hall made clear to architect Tom Croce was their desire for good light in the tack-up and grooming stalls. Here Rodgers grooms Aequus, the most successful park horse in the history of the breed, with eight national championships. Raegan Knotts readies Pete for exercise in the arena.

it would do in a moderate winter even if we have a typical one with 0 or 10 degrees in January."

"John was adamant about using a forced-air heating system," Croce said. "We had to make sure we maintained the air quality. Usually people say they need a lot of ventilation. But 'ventilation' often is the remedy for bad air quality. And that opens up other topics and questions: Where do you store hay and bedding? If they're in a loft overhead, there's fire risk and ever-present dust. Here they're in a separate building. How often are stalls cleaned? Are the animals in the stalls during cleaning, stirring up the dust?

"John worked in Wisconsin where dairy farmers use the PATS system to remove manure from milking stations. This mechanized metal conveyor system operates in the floor or under it. He liked the idea of shoveling the shavings and manure

down an opening rather than tossing it into the air towards a wheelbarrow. But we had to devise something to accommodate a trap door [to shovel the manure and shavings through] that would not stick open and injure a horse. We made a small structure in the stall that holds water and feed bowls, and we store each horse's halter on the outside of the stall.

"The heating system was the real challenge. If you run a hundred feet of ductwork in an unheated space, that duct will fill with cold air. When the fan starts, before any heat reaches the stalls, you're blowing cold air onto the animals which creates a draft that can cause potential problems. We came up with a system that heated water and circulated it through pumps to fan-coil boxes. Each box heats three stalls. We bring the supply air for the heaters in through the dormers. Exhaust air is controlled through the cupolas which are tied to the

Ronita, Freedom Farm's largest Dutch harness mare, exhales protectively over her yearling daughter, Duchess of Hazelbank, sired by Aequus. Here Judi Lee, farm manager, leads Ronita while Dave Sweitzer escorts her offspring to one of the farm's turnout pastures.

heating system. We even put ammonia sensors in the stalls for those nights that are too warm to need heat but too cool to open dormers or doors. The sensors read air quality and will kick on the exhaust fans in the cupolas if levels climb too high. This system is very sophisticated but when you look at the total cost of the barn, it didn't add that much more to it."

"In the winters," Hall said, "we want to create the circumstance where the horse cools off overnight to keep it healthy. They grow their winter coats. During the daytime they come out of their 45 degree stalls and into the 50 degree arena. They go around a couple of times, warm up, and they can go through an exercise program without feeling stressed. It goes back to our premise here, as Bill Rodgers will tell you, 'A comfortable horse will learn.' If we create an environment where the horse is happy and has everything else going for it, you get that glorious circumstance where the horse is willing to learn and ready to go out there and try its best.

"The ones that are superstars in this barn have tremendously strong personalities. They are very self-assured. They live for the moment when everybody else has to leave the arena and they have the roses and ribbons around their necks and they do the victory lap by themselves. They may not have quite the same level of complex reasoning and analytical skills that we have but they have remarkable memories. Amazing abilities to relate situations, and they do have the same characteristics as the human animals do."

In many ways, Freedom Farm is a state-of-the-art facility. The research that John Hall and Bill Rodgers do in horse training, health, and safety continues on a daily basis. At Freedom Farm, Hall has developed SUCCEED Digestive Conditioning Program™, a daily use product that allows the horse to digest normally to retain or regain internal health for maximum performance. SUCCEED™ was the second business to grow out of Freedom Farm. Meanwhile Tom Croce's knowledge expands as his business becomes more oriented toward equine clients, a conscious direction change he made in 2005.

"Our relationship with the horse has changed from them being used as a work animal to being used for pleasure and as a hobby," Croce explained. "A lot of the stabling has changed to reflect that. Instead of the necessity to keep the animals protected, now it is a luxury to have a place to house our horses. The animal is so darned accommodating that we now understand that we were doing things to them that not only were not ideal but that might even have hurt them. Our information has gotten better about the needs of horses, about what we need to do to keep them healthier and happier."

Raegan works with Pete in Freedom Farm's 100x200-foot indoor arena while Rodgers rides Aequus. The bright, airy structure uses three 8-foot bladed ceiling fans to circulate air. The footing material is polymerized (plastic-coated) sand to provide horses an ideal Clegg Impact (essentially a bounce rating) score of 125.

Round Lot Farm
Medfield, Massachusetts

Architectural Elegance in New England

"My mother grew up riding," Ros Smythe said. "I come from a family of eight kids and I was the only one of us who had the horse bug so I had lessons when I was little."

When the family housekeeper quit, Ros' mother seized an opportunity. Instead of hiring another housekeeper, she did the work, paying herself what she previously had paid someone else. By the time Ros was in seventh grade, her mom had bought her a horse from the household savings.

"The horse we bought was pregnant so within a year I had two horses!"

Ros competed in local shows, never chasing the larger dreams of the big shows. She rode constantly through high school, college, and graduate school.

"Then when I got out of graduate school, I went to work and I quit riding," she explained. "We lived in New York, then in San Francisco, and then just outside of Boston. And then my husband made the mistake of saying, 'Ros, you've been a good wife and you've worked hard for us all. If you want to go follow this horse thing now, you can.'

"I said, 'Great!' I bought a horse. We already were looking for a larger house. I didn't like the way the stable was caring for my horse and I couldn't find anywhere that had the care I was looking for. So we started looking for a house with options for a barn."

The place they found, 30 acres farther outside Boston, already had a barn. Below the barn, a few cows were living in a quagmire of mud and cow waste products. Ros described it as pretty disgusting and gross. She and her husband, Dan, envisioned a new barn and an enclosed arena. They would use the old barn as a temporary stable while someone built their new one.

Ros Smythe's asymmetrical shingle-style barn makes an elegant backdrop for her easy workout on her 15-year old Dutch Warmblood Ermitina K, better known as Queen.

For Ros Smythe, her husband, Dan, and their architect, John Blackburn, their 1914 brick Georgian-style home in the background provided a bit of trouble as they conceived the horse barn for the property. Ros had no desire for a brick barn or Georgian formality.

Ros found an ad in a horse journal for John Blackburn in Washington, D.C. They had a house architect who loved barns and horses and whose daughter rode. But he admitted that in building a barn, there are things you have to know that he didn't.

"First we did a master plan of their land," John Blackburn recalled. "Ros wanted a barn and an arena because she was going to get back into serious riding and then competition. Our original plan put the barn and arena on the other side of the house from where the barn is. But there was a neighbor back there and Dan was concerned about the big building he would see everyday.

"Their home is Georgian style, built of red brick. While we were doing the design work, we originally started with a bit of brick, to relate to the house. But I didn't want to do a Georgian barn because that's not what is around their area. I traveled around that part of Massachusetts and all the other structures, barns, outbuildings, and houses were either Cape Cod or shingle style. The decision to go with shingle style came from the Smythes. It meshed with their needs, it meshed with the existing barn, and it really was based on a mixture of things. My mantra while planning and designing a barn is to consider the needs of the horse, the goals of the client, and the demands of the site."

The barn was not structurally sound, but neither Ros nor her husband knew barns. They had a contractor, Doug Whitla, whom they asked to look at the barn with an idea of remodeling it. He took a look and to dramatize his conclusions, he pushed his fist easily through a wall, telling them, "This is a waste." That ended any plan to make temporary use of it, and Whitla's demonstration directly affected the new barn's location.

Blackburn asked Ros countless questions to determine what she wanted. She thought she'd need three or four stalls

On a cool, gray evening, the barn glows warmly and inviting after its daily activities are complete. Architect John Blackburn specified white cedar shingles for siding and red cedar for the roof.

but everyone she spoke with, from friends to competitors to past Olympians, from whom she took workshops, told her to take her original estimate and always add two or four more. She told Blackburn she wanted a barn that was easy to work and easy to work in. She wanted a tack room that might double as an office. She wanted a laundry.

"I didn't know enough to know what else I wanted. But John continued to ask questions and figure out what's going to work for me and be useful. He wanted to know what I wanted my aisle made out of. What did I want in the bottom of the horses' stall?

"We have asphalt and then rubber on top of that, which is maintenance-free in the extreme. The aisles have drains in them, which are great. John specified the type of tarmac in there. You can't have anything too slippery for the horses, because with their shoes on, they will slip. And you want something porous so if you spill or splash water when it's cold in New England, it freezes, and it can stay there for two or three days. You've created an ice-slick in your barn, which is not only an equine safety hazard but also one for humans. There are things like that that John thinks of and they're really useful."

Blackburn carried on the story during an interview in his office in Washington, D.C. "Ros told me that she was going to have a woman in to run the barn. But occasionally she was going to be out there feeding, mucking stalls, and tending the horses, and she wanted it easy to work in." All of that he easily could accommodate, but he offered more.

"I tell every client," he continued, "that when you're ready to design a barn, our goal in working with you is to find the social

When Ros conceived her barn, she thought three or four stalls would be adequate. She met an ex-Olympian who told her, "Take the number of stalls you think you need, add two or four more, and you're going to be fine." She settled on eight.

Lucas Equine Equipment's stall fronts and doors allow the horses to keep an eye on each other. The doors permit owners or stable hands to see quickly if horses are okay or are down.

center for that barn. Every barn has a social center. One reason is that more horse people are women than men and they are more social than we are. They communicate; they talk about their horses, their children, their jobs, and other things too. Where do they do this is the question we want to answer. Well, they talk in the stalls, in the wash stall, in the grooming area, they do it in the tack room, they do it in an office, they do it in a lounge. Every barn is different; every client is different, and my goal is to find out where your social center needs to be."

Ros had a plan that if her trainer worked out, she might run a small sales operation out of an office in the barn. She has added horses and rides every day but the sales opportunity hasn't come together. Yet soon after Blackburn and contractor Doug Whitla finished the barn, Dan spent several months working from home in the sunny, inviting office/tack room.

Ros and Dan found a great method to insure barn completion by a set date. They planned a party for the contractor, subcontractors, and their crews, set a date, invited everyone, and put up a calendar inside the barn counting down to the party night. No one was late, either on completion, or to the party.

Outside, the barn is finished in white cedar shingles. The roof shingles are red cedar. Interior walls are fir bead board with pine flooring in the office/tack room. Stall doors and grilles came from Lucas Equine Equipment in Cynthiana, Kentucky.

With her other horses turned out, Ros grooms Queen in the well-located and brightly lit wash stall before her ride. The stalls are surfaced with asphalt with a layer of rubber on top, and the stall fronts are powder coated.

With its boot tree stretching it tall, a single riding boot stands like decoration in a window of the tack room/lounge. Ros Smythe wanted a comfortable room for sitting or for working her horse brokerage.

The large tack room functions as an office, conference room, equipment storage, tack cleaning area, kitchen, laundry, and bathroom. A ramshackle barn stood on the site before new construction began and from it the Smythes could save only the brass bridle hangers.

Winter sun streams through Lucas'
window hardware and casts
shadows on the high stall sidewalls.
Fixed clerestory windows above the
Lucas grilles bring in additional light,
as well as faithfully representing
shingle-style architecture.

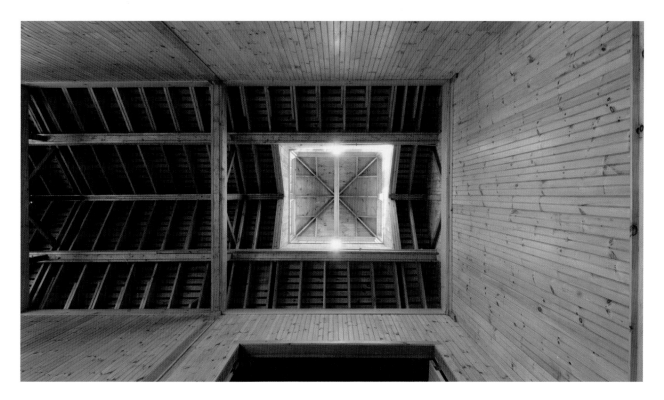

Fir bead board lines the upper atrium up to the cupola. Double doors open to one of two accesses to the upstairs feed and bedding storage loft. The other is from the outside where suppliers use long conveyors to lift supplies.

The second floor of the barn houses a spacious but unfinished living area and a larger hay loft with storage for bedding as well. This one is tightly sealed to contain dust. Each of the light fixtures not only is dust-proof, but at the county electrical inspector's insistence, each is in an explosion-proof housing. All the wiring is encased in conduits. Even hay and bedding delivery minimizes dust in the barn. The suppliers run a long conveyor up from their truck through the hay door on the end of the barn rather than tracking it through the building and up.

Ros and Dan Smythe and John Blackburn look back on the barn-building experience with pleasant memories. "John has told me that we were one of his easiest barns to work on," Ros recalled. "Between dealing with the contractor and the owner, there usually is some major issue. We didn't have that."

"I think it's a tribute to the relationships between the client and the architect," Blackburn said. "We've had nice clients and not-so-nice clients. But this barn is the result of great clients with great attitude and respect for what we do."

Ros has added horses to her stable. She now has four, two of which are resting through the winter while the other two get gentle daily workouts every day except when fresh snow covers the pasture in front of the barn. Her children are growing; her oldest is in college and her youngest has turned 14 and is applying to boarding high schools. Ros wrestles with what happens next.

"What I think will happen is, well, I'll begin to do stuff to get busy again . . . . I think." She laughed. She says she'll ride

much more and perhaps start chasing the dreams of the bigger shows. "But all the decisions on the barn are up to me. All the decisions on the property are pretty much up to me. The vast majority of the decisions on the house are my decisions. My husband, Dan, works. I like running my own property. I like having this. This is my barn."

At the rear of the barn, a large balcony off the office/tack room hangs out over the two-door, double-depth garage to look out over a planned arena. Space exists on the top floor for a spacious apartment as housing for a potential live-in trainer.

Caper Lea Stables
Trappe, Maryland

Intimacy and Innovation
on Maryland's Eastern Shore

It's been Carey Miller's dream for 30 years. For 25 years, she has worked to make her dream—and the barn in her imagination—an income-producing business. She and Peter Zukoski found their land 20 years ago and pooled their funds to make her dream happen.

The driving force in Carey's life has been her passion for animals, living with them, and surrounding herself with natural open spaces. Getting to her dream, and enduring the occasional interruptions, has been an interesting journey. At the time they met, Miller, who was a classically trained cellist from Delaware, was working as a crop specialist with a leading agricultural retail supplier based in the Midwest. Her education at Cornell University had led her to doing field work studying animal behavior in the Rift Valley of central Kenya, Africa, for five years following up her schooling. Back in the United States, and with a few years' experience selling fertilizer, she missed the animal interaction and she was ready to go to school to become a farrier.

Zukoski was a university-trained furniture designer and master woodworker from Rochester, New York, who had taught himself classical guitar in the early 1960s, because no school in the United States offered a major program for it then. He made his living renovating old boats and building new ones, work that included spending a couple of years in China coordinating an export yacht-building facility.

When they first met, Peter was teaching classical guitar in a studio in Easton, Maryland, and Carey was rehearsing with a newly formed string quartet in the same building. A few years later when they met again, she

Carey Miller leads Ninja, an Arabian/Saddlebred cross, out of her spacious octagonal barn. Miller, a farrier and horse massage practitioner, operates her farm as a short-term boarding and rest and rehabilitation facility for her clients.

Ninja enjoys a morning snack in one of the turnouts. The barn, measuring 48 feet across, provides six large trapezoid-shaped stalls and a guest room above the large central aisle.

had a horse, a dog, and a cat, and couldn't put together how she could attend farrier school out of state and care for the animals.

"And then I came along," Peter said with a laugh.

"I started taking horse-riding lessons when I was seven," Carey explained. "I didn't have my own horse, but I took lessons. For two of the five years I was in Africa, I lived on a wheat farm and looked after five horses there. They let me borrow one of their horses and that felt like the first horse I could call my own."

Carey showed horses briefly as a youth. She had a solid foundation in classical riding instruction long before moving to Africa. But riding in Kenya, over that kind of terrain, with giraffes, watching out for aardvark holes, was something special.

After returning to the United States, she had adopted her first horse, Rosie. While Peter took care of her pets, Carey attended Danny Ward's Eastern School of Farriery in Martinsville, Virginia. It took little time to get her new business going and she came to specialize "in people who have

horses as pets." It was about that time that she and Peter began looking at property and contemplating her barn. They named the parcel they found, 34 wooded acres on the eastern shore of the Chesapeake, "Caper Lea," mixing parts of their first names with the noun for a meadow or pasture in the woods.

"The idea was to have a barn and a boarding facility," she explained, "at first to augment the farrier business and then one day to *be* the business. At first we were thinking of something that would have 30 horses. Huge. That was unreasonable. Maybe a dream. Maybe a nightmare now that I know more about it," she said.

"As we came to our senses over the years, we scaled down our ideas. We spent a number of years just talking about what it was going to look like. Every spring we'd go on a three-day

trip and look at other places. I wanted Peter to see the kind of place I had in mind so that we wouldn't be building some place that was like everybody else's, meaning square.

"We talked about doing a barn that was U-shaped, with a courtyard. We had an opportunity to get free trusses for some sort of rectangular thing. But we were always going back to the fact that you could get more under one roof for the amount of siding and structure with a round building. And it's strong."

"It started out as a 12-sided barn," Peter recalled. "It would have been twice the size of the barn that's there now. It would have been three stories tall instead of two. It would have been 7,500 square feet. With that plan we could have had 12 stalls, 8 around the edges with 4 in the center.

Miller's husband, Peter Zukoski, a master boat-builder by profession, designed and constructed the barn based on Miller's requirements. To be certain that angles worked, he assembled a scale model before beginning the full-scale work.

While the horse gets morning treats, Carey Miller's Australian cattle dog, Ziggy, hopes something will fall his way. Each of the six stalls opens in to a central hexagonal enclosure, as well as out to the surrounding pastures.

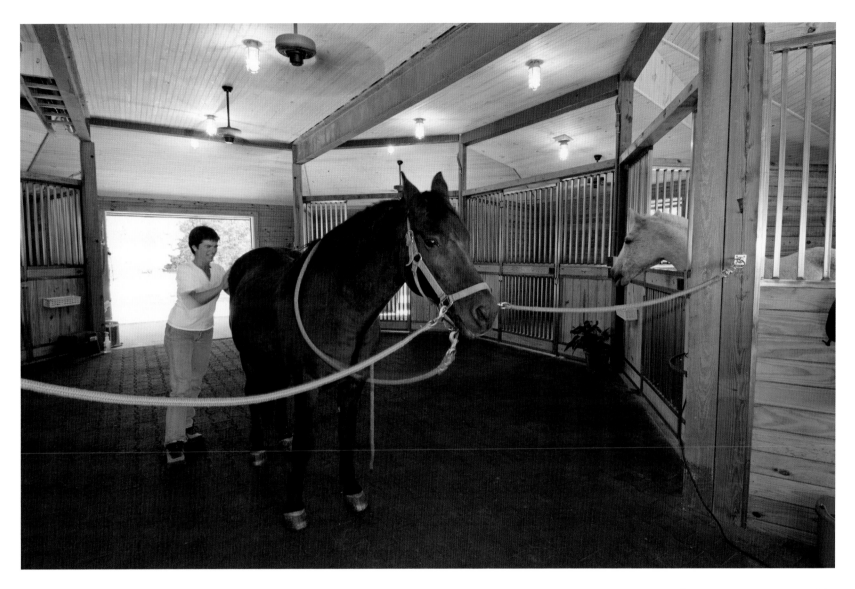

"We got back to reality," he continued. "We built one of these little run-in sheds. The polygons really came from Carey talking about the round stuff she'd seen in Africa. I liked the idea, but I wasn't going to start steam-bending wood to make a round anything."

What Peter did do was make a quarter-inch scale model using balsa-wood sticks and a hot glue gun. He built the structure, working out the construction details in three dimensions. They liked what he had conceived so he made a larger model, and then made prints from that. He does his designs on the computer and he did lofting drawings of some of the roof forms, just as he does when designing a boat.

"Construction took seven years," Peter said. But that was not seven years nonstop. "I built the equipment shed, and two other buildings while that was going on. Run-in sheds, Carey's office. The equipment shed, and fencing." Meanwhile, Carey

kept up a daunting client load that sometimes meant shoeing 350 horses on a regular schedule.

The barn contracted to an octagon with six stalls. From flat wall across the barn to flat wall measures 48 feet on the ground floor. An upstairs studio 24 feet across is where Carey teaches cello and guests stay the night. They moved the first horses in on Christmas Eve 2003.

The trapezoidal stalls measure 12 feet wide inside the barn, 12 feet deep, and 20 feet along the outside walls. When Peter and Carey talked with stall equipment salespeople, they balked at the quotes they received. Peter knew a scrapyard in Delaware. He hired a friend and bought a mig welder and 2,000 pounds of stainless tubing in two sizes. They set up a pattern jig in his equipment shed. He and his friend turned out all the stall doors, walls, and sidewalls for less than $6,000, including the price of the welder and wages for their friend.

Miller gives Lassiter, a 21-year old Morgan, a vigorous grooming in the center of the barn. Ceiling fans and wide doorways in the path of prevailing winds keep fresh air moving inside the barn. Interlocking rubber bricks provide comfortable and sure footing.

Carey set up the barn as a boarding stable, not for tenants who would ride on the farm, but for her farrier clients who needed a place to keep their horses when they left town. Along the way to her goal, she and Peter married. She continues moving toward making her farm a lay-up, rest, and rehabilitation facility for horses.

She aimed to become the "best horse hoof professional" in her area. She studied whole-horse anatomy extensively. "The hoof is a prime case of form follows function," she said, "so keeping the rest of the body functional will allow the feet to come into functional form as well. Then what follows is the importance of saddle fit and ultimately rider posture." She has expanded her newer expertise in horse massage. She began taking anatomy courses in 1994 and did workshops and clinics. She started massaging professionally in 1997, the same year she and Peter broke ground on the barn. Just like her farrier business did, this new enterprise has caught on.

"I have a steady repeat business," she explained. "Their horses like it here. They're very relaxed. The stalls are large, open. The horses can see into the alley or out to the rest of the farm." Their floor plan leaves ample room in the rubber-brick-floored center of the barn. She easily can work on a horse

(left) The barn gives horses ample opportunity for socializing. Stall side walls are partially grilled, affording some privacy to horses easily intimidated during feeding. The high, bright ceilings bounce around a great deal of light. Paneling is loblolly pine.

(below) While one of Miller's tenants eats, another stares curiously at the camera. While the inside stall wall is 12 feet, the trapezoidal shape created by 12-foot diagonal side walls and 20-foot-long outside walls provides spacious accommodation. The stall doors feature removable upper sections to allow horses to look around in the barn.

(above) Miller's intimate six-stall barn allows her to provide intense personal attention to each of her boarders. The large center of the barn offers Miller, a trained farrier and horse massage practitioner, space to attend to horse's feet and to relax and release tight muscles, which are services available to any of her guests.

(right) Caper Lea Farm offers grassy and sand turnouts for its guests. Miller moved her first horses in on Christmas Eve 2003.

In the late afternoon sun, Miller leads Ninja back to the barn from one of the grassy turnouts. Caper Lea Farm is on the eastern shore of Chesapeake Bay.

(below) While Carey Miller looks on, her husband, Peter Zukoski, explains a detail of the octagonal barn floor plan. Behind them is a sailboat he will restore and renovate for a client.

without risking injury to the animal or herself if it moves. "And the owners even can sign up their horses for massage therapy during their stay," she added.

Most of her clients see a difference in their horses. She likens her technique to a deep-muscle "grooming." Equine stress will tighten muscles that affect the horse's movement. One symptom can be a horse frequently throwing—or stepping off—its shoes. The forelegs are stiff enough that they do not get out of the way of the rears, or vice versa. "Performance athletes," she said, "are subject to the same muscular stress whether their muscles are in a human body or a horse body. These muscles are going to take a beating, and need care, rest, and tissue manipulation.

"It's all about deep muscle manipulation, but it's really determined by what the horses can tolerate. Some horses you can only barely touch. This is sophisticated grooming without the brushes. But many owners don't have the time to do that anymore. People don't groom their horses unless they're going to ride, and most people don't ride every day.

"I do that for my guests. I do that for my own horses. I think that's why my 35-year-old Rosie is still here and limber. When I have horses here for boarding, I treat them like they're my own and I treat them as if they're the only horse here. They get thoroughly groomed twice a day. They get spa-like treatment."

Chesapeake Dressage Institute
Annapolis, Maryland

Classical Training within Classical Architecture

"I call my horses my Zen masters," Janet Richardson-Pearson explained. "They are the one place in my life where trying hard to give it my all doesn't always give me the results I expect. You have to sit back and relax and let things happen. Trying to make them happen has worked in other areas of my life but it hasn't worked in this one."

Janet never sat on a horse until she was 35. However, in the years since she took her first lesson with her young daughter, Jennifer, she has approached the sport of dressage with a dedication that has become passionate.

Riding was something she always wanted to do, but she married young, had children early, went to school, and then began a career as a commercial interior designer. For more than 17 years she planned offices, ever larger and more complex, always studying what needed to be where and making certain it got there. When her daughter was old enough, they began taking lessons on a regular basis with different trainers in the area. Then Linda Zang opened a dressage training facility in southern Maryland. Zang was a U.S. Olympic team competitor cheated out of her chance for gold in 1980 by the international politics that kept the American team from going to Moscow.

Zang's students could ride and take lessons through the winters and in bad weather because Idlewilde Farm in Davidsonville, Maryland, where she taught, had a covered indoor arena. Janet took a lesson a week for years until her children were older. Then she finally bought her own horse. She lived on a property with a small pasture, kept her horse at home, and her trainer came there for lessons. With friends and neighbors

Owner Janet Richardson-Pearson describes her facility as a kind of "equestrian learning research center." She concentrates primarily on dressage discipline and training.

she rode the trails in her area for another few years until suburban development swallowed up her rural surroundings. She moved her horse to a trainer's barn, and boarded and took lessons there for quite a few more years. But she grew tired of hauling her horse to clinics and lessons. She decided to bring her animal home and to build a facility where she and others could progress as riders and become more serious about their dressage training and skills.

Janet began to plan her future facility. Her daughter, Jennifer, now a successful local dressage competitor, and her husband, Michael, together operate Equestrian Services, LLC, an Annapolis, Maryland–based equestrian site-planning and arena-development firm. They helped Janet locate architect Ravi Waldron and contractors, Hogg Construction who could execute her plan.

Janet had traveled for several years to the shows and competitions in Wellington, Florida, in late winter. Equestrian estates pepper the area, some of which are open to visitors during show season. Janet toured farms and took photos of the barns and arenas she admired. She gave her collection of pictures to Waldron to show him what she wanted.

She had a long riding history by this time and she had visited enough barns to know very clearly what she wanted. In her years as a commercial interior designer planning office

Owner Janet Richardson-Pearson finished a lesson and workout on Gaspar, her Dutch Warmblood, in her arena. The insulated but unheated arena has roll-up windows to catch prevailing winds during warmer months.

Architect Ravi Waldron, recognizing the importance of good air quality and ventilation, as well as good light, designed a series of visually interesting cupolas and monitor roof vents atop the barn and arena.

Trainer Cheryl Garrido rides Fortune, a Hanerovian. Her husband, Marcelo, works behind her, teasing Fortune's rear legs with a light whip, training the horse to do Piaffe, an Olympic-level dressage maneuver sometimes described as "trot in place."

spaces, she had created hundreds of building layouts. She knew where she wanted her tack room, where the tack-up areas and the wash stalls should be, where she would put her manager's office and residence, and where the lounge and viewing area had to go. She created the barn concept and plan herself and turned her work over to Waldron to complete. What she needed next were people to manage the barn, train her horses, and teach her the skills she knew she needed.

"One of my crucial goals was to have someone working here who had European training, was an upper-level rider, and had experience training people to move up the levels," she explained. "*Dressage* is a French word for 'training,' but the origin of the discipline goes back to Alexander the Great. A lot of the classical techniques of training the horse go back that far. And that's what I wanted to do here, to teach the classical dressage movements, but using some of the innovative learning techniques."

Janet established the Chesapeake Dressage Institute, and the county stepped in to ensure that, even as a not-for-profit organization, her "business" facility complied with strict safety

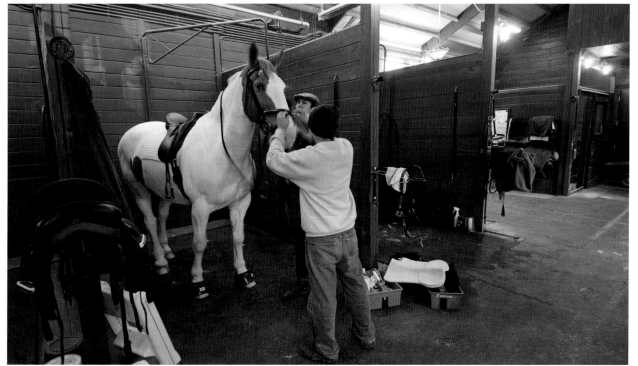

During morning cleanup, stable hands and grooms work over the barn's 16 stalls. Feed and bedding storage is above the center aisle. The barn houses owner Richardson-Pearson's horses, as well as those of boarders who take riding and dressage instruction from trainer Cheryl Garrido and visiting instructors.

The educational nature of the barn dictated three grooming and tacking stalls. The warm coffee-brown walls complement the bright, airy barn. Interlocking rubber pads provide comfort and sure-footing for horses, riders, and stable staff.

Sunlight streams in the south-facing front windows as staff members finish the morning clean up. Richardson-Pearson had very specific requirements for her architect as far as interior configuration and exterior appearance were concerned.

and fire codes. While it is a board-and-batten wood barn faithfully designed and built to Janet's specification, there are sprinklers in the manager's apartment and fire doors separate segments of the structure from one another. The arena, which she describes as a "barn on steroids," was based on specific structures she saw in Wellington. Like Zang's indoor facility, this one allows her, her trainer, and her boarders to ride and train year-round.

"When times have been tough, the barn has always been my refuge," Janet said. "Horses are wonderfully giving animals. It's amazing what they let people do to them. They are prey animals; that's why they bolt and run. That's their only defense, mainly, against the big meateaters. Yet they let humans sit on their backs. They give themselves to us to carry our burdens.

"We're looking at ways to provide the best training possible here for the horse and for the rider, classical ways, no shortcuts. People in the education field have discovered that people learn in different ways. That's another thing we're doing here with our center is working to find ways to teach people that suit their own learning styles. Dressage is a method of training with expected results.

"We work on the mind-body connection and in fitness areas so that you have a unification, a partnership in which you are dancing with your horse," she continued. At her Chesapeake Dressage Institute, she regularly schedules riding and training clinics with past U.S. Olympic team riders and other top-level international riders and instructors. The facility hosts workshops on horse nutrition, saddle fitting, sports psychology, and rider fitness.

"We're a kind of equestrian learning research center," Janet explained. "We want to be a place that promotes really good dressage. Performance horses today get dental visits every year, they have chiropractors, get massages, use special farriers, and eat nutritional food. Performance horses today get the same treatment that top-level human athletes receive."

Highest level dressage for the rider requires balance and fitness. Subtlety of movement, mostly in the seat and leg, communicates with the horse very effectively. To that end, Richardson-Pearson has begun hosting Pilates workshops, as well as yoga, tai chi, weight training, and aerobics at her farm. In fact, her only regret with the traditional 14-stall barn design is it lacks an additional room for Pilates and other fitness and exercise classes.

"Basically," Janet said, "my concept is to utilize the body-mind-spirit experience and to be the best you can be in your riding, which spills over into the rest of your life. The journey of horse ownership, riding, and training has led me down very interesting paths just because I wanted to be a better rider. It's been an interesting journey of discovery."

One recent visitor ventured to define her Chesapeake Dressage Institute as the integration of equine well-being and human well-being. Janet has a better characterization for what she does and what appeals to her about it.

"My husband said when I was getting dressed for a competition that the process sort of reminded him of the ceremonies of the matadors as they dress before the bullfight. It does sort of have symbolic meaning.

"Some people don't like this remark, but I always say, 'Dressage is the perfect sport for obsessive compulsive perfectionists.'"

Garrido works Fortune through a range of dressage maneuvers. She exercises each horse in the barn six days a week in the 20x60-meter regulation arena.

(above) The daily duties board shows the sequence for the Institute's stable staff to have horses tacked-up and ready for riders and training. At 7:35 a.m. on a mid-November morning, the fresh-air-filled barn showed 33 degrees on the thermometer.

(right) The cleverly designed tack room complex features several lockers and several larger walk-in closets, such as this one for boarders. The tack room also has a changing room, laundry, and shower.

(far right) Marcelo Garrido leads his horse Soloman off the barn's front porch to a smaller stable after finishing an arena training ride and outdoor exercise session. Concealed under the porch eaves is one of many remotely controlled monitors and security closed-circuit cameras.

Casa Loma
Toronto, Ontario

Sir Henry Pellatt's Equestrian Castle

His personal motto was *Devant, si je puis*, French for "Foremost, if I can." Henry Mill Pellatt lived that motto to the fullest, especially in the case of his home and his stables near downtown Toronto. Born in Windsor, Ontario, in 1859, he was the first of seven children. His father moved them to Toronto when Henry was just 2, and started a stock brokerage when his oldest son was 7. At 17, young Henry graduated from Upper Canada College and set off to see the world. He fell in love with European traditions and architecture, especially those related to royalty and the military. Traveling through the countryside, he made drawings and sketches of the great castles he visited, building a file he hoped someday he would use.

Back home in Toronto, he entered his father's brokerage, and a year later at 18 he joined the local regiment of the Queen's Own Rifles, practicing nights and weekends to learn the drills and routines of the horse-mounted cavalry unit. An adept horseman, he won the Dominion Mile at age 19, a harness race contested on July 1, Dominion Day, across Canada. Within four years he had married his sweetheart, Mary Dodgson, a well-connected local society girl. As a wedding present, his father named him a partner in the brokerage and renamed the firm Pellatt & Pellatt.

Henry wasted no time jumping to the forefront of innovation and business adventure. In 1883, at age 24, he founded the Toronto Electric Light Co., (TELC) in the new Victoria Tin Works Building on Sherbourne Street. His partnership with his father gave him the entrée and polish to entice investors, and he won the contract to install 32 street lights through downtown Toronto. Six years later, TELC obtained a 30-year exclusive

Sir Henry Pellat's carriage house and stables betray his abiding interest in Gothic and medieval architecture. Designed by E. J. Lennox and constructed by Herbert Elgie starting in 1905, elaborate decoration befits the castle Sir Henry had in mind. *Donna Griffith*

The barn complex is a masterpiece of Gothic/Mannerist decoration with towers, turrets, conical roofs, and stepped gables. Sir Henry Pellat's family crest crowns the doors, flanked by heraldic horses.

Architect E. J. Lennox fulfilled Sir Henry Pellat's fantasy of a Mannerist castle for Sir Henry's horses. Construction cost was reported at $250,000 at the time, which is between $4 and $5 million today.

agreement to supply street lighting to the city. It launched his fortune. He expanded his electric enterprises to Sao Paulo and later Rio de Janeiro, Brazil, founding tram and electric power companies in both cities.

Coal-powered generators cost too much in raw materials and river power was more efficient. In 1903 Pellatt and three partners launched the Electrical Development Company of Ontario and built Canada's first hydroelectric generating station at Niagara Falls. His fortune grew exponentially. He invested in the Canadian Pacific Railroad and bought all the stock that he could in the Canada Northwest Land Company. Within a few years, he had accumulated between $3 million and $4 million, which is equivalent to $100 million today. During this time he had continued his involvement with the Queen's Own Rifles, rising to the rank of lieutenant colonel. Through his participation in this organization and his business efforts that electrified eastern Canada, he was knighted by England's King Edward VII and became Sir Henry Pellatt in 1905.

It was close enough to royalty for Pellatt, and soon after he began to unfurl his old drawings of European castles along with his imagination. Wise enough to know the fickle nature of good fortune, he acquired 25 estate lots at the top of Davenport Hill in his wife's name. This would be the site for his own castle, Casa Loma, Spanish for "house on a hill." In 1903 he had hired the city's foremost architect, Edward Lennox, who had done

Six large standing stalls of mahogany lined one side of the stable while three double-size foaling boxes filled the other wall. Sir Henry imported Spanish tiles for the herringbone-patterned floor.
Donna Griffith

countless commercial and municipal buildings. Pellatt handed him his collection of drawings and sketches and said, "Design me a castle!"

Lennox bought himself a lot near the site, designed his own home and studio, and set out to fulfill Pellatt's dream. He began planning construction of stables, a carriage house, grooms' and stable hands' quarters, a conservatory, and Pellatt's temporary residence, the Hunting Lodge. Herbert Elgie, Lennox's trusted contractor, began construction in 1905. Lennox conceived a small castle for the stables, derived from Norman and Scottish influences, with crenellations (slots in the top for archers to fire down onto invaders) and punctuated with Gothic details everywhere.

Pellatt owned Thoroughbreds, Hackneys, Clydesdales, and Percherons. For his efforts with the Queens' Own Rifles, he owned two chargers, Prince Highgate and The Widow. Lennox designed a central courtyard in front of an L-shaped building constructed of red brick and Credit Valley stone. Horse activities came and went through the north doorway. A foyer opened to six large, open standing stalls on one side and three very large box stalls opposite. Lennox faced each of these with Spanish mahogany. Pellatt imported pale green and red glazed tiles from Spain, the colors of his beloved Queen's Own Rifles. Herringbone brickwork covered the stable floors to lessen

Pellat was deeply proud of his participation in the Queen's Own Rifles to such an extent that he ordered his barn decorated in ceramic wall tiles in the green and red colors of the regiment. Each standing stall featured the gold-gilt name of its inhabitant.
Donna Griffith

Sir Henry's grooms brought horses into the stables from either end of the room. Brass rods pulled out from each walk-in stall and attached to the box stalls opposite to help direct the animal into its own stall. *Donna Griffith*

The carriage room is an imposing and dramatically scaled storage area. Clear-span oak trusses support the high ceiling. Pellat sold his carriages when the mansion was auctioned. These belong to Toronto-area collectors for display purposes. *Donna Griffith*

the risk of a horse slipping. Pellatt had Elgie hire a gold-leaf engraver who embossed the names of his favorite horses at the head of their stalls. A large 37x42-foot carriage room opened straight through the foyer. The tack room sat opposite the stables. A garage for Pellatt's growing collection of automobiles opened onto the courtyard as well.

Elgie completed the stable complex in 1906 at a cost reported to be $250,000 (somewhere between $4 million and $5 million today). Pellatt moved into the Hunting Lodge a hundred yards away and watched as Elgie and Lennox began construction of his 98-room castle. To further refine his ideas, and to be sure his architect understood what he wanted, Pellatt took Lennox with him on a long trip to Europe and Great Britain to see other structures and to begin to acquire furniture, artwork, and other treasures for the home.

Local politicians began challenging his monopoly on city lighting and power. Cabinet minister Adam Beck, elected on a platform of reducing electric costs, set up the Hydro Production

The upper-level hay loft provided storage for hundreds of tons of feed and bedding. The doors gave access for a conveyor to elevate supplies up to the loft. *Donna Griffith*

Upper floors of the castle-like stables and carriage house provided apartments and sleeping rooms for grooms, stable hands, and carriage drivers. This lighthouse-like spiral staircase was the only access to the rooms. *Donna Griffith*

Architect E. J. Lennox and builder Herbert Elgie understood the weights and stresses of hundreds of tons of feed and bedding materials. Elgie constructed the building using poured concrete, heavy steel beams, and post-and-beam timber frame technologies. *Donna Griffith*

This was the main room of the head groomsman's spacious apartment. One large radiator keeps the apartment warm in Toronto winters. The floors are red oak.
Donna Griffith

Power Commission and demanded public ownership of utilities such as Pellatt's Electric Development Company. Despite these substantial threats to his wealth, Pellatt continued to spend money like water flowing over Niagara Falls. In 1906 Sir Henry transported 900 men and their equipment to New York City's Madison Square Garden for a military show. This earned him promotion to colonel. In 1910, on the 50th anniversary of the unit, Sir Henry took 640 officers and men, all their horses and equipment to England for month-long war games in August. The trip cost him as much as his stables: $250,000. For this, Sir Henry received the Commander of Victorian Order (CVO) from King George V while he and his unit were there.

Lennox and Elgie began construction of the castle home in 1909 and, to some extent, just like George Vanderbilt's Ashville, and William Randolph Hearst's San Simeon, the owner, architect, and builder never really completed it. Pellatt and his wife moved into the house in 1913, as construction continued around them. Sir Henry had asked the city to close a street in front of his castle between it, his gardens, and the stables. The city refused, so Elgie constructed an 800-foot long tunnel between the two that served Pellatt far better in the cold Toronto winters.

Pellatt's horses, Matchless and Lord Kitchener, often won in show rings. He acquired a 445-acre farm near Lake Marie north of Toronto to begin a horse breeding operation. His stable manager, Thomas Cushing, trained many of Pellatt's horses as winners in dressage, flat track racing, and show jumping.

Pellatt's money ran out in 1923. He declared bankruptcy and moved to the Lake Marie Farm. Between 1925 and 1928, the castle was converted to an apartment hotel. Guests and neighbors boarded their horses in the stables. In 1936 the Kiwanis Club of West Toronto was able to lease the entire estate from the City of Toronto, which had acquired it from Pellatt for nonpayment of property taxes. The Kiwanis opened the estate a year later to the public and it remains the club's property to this date. Sir Henry died in 1939.

Biltmore Historic Horse Barn
Asheville, North Carolina

George Vanderbilt's Working Horse Barn

Some historians say that the Vanderbilt family created "The Golden Era." This period of six decades from the late 1800s into the early 1900s is best known for the fantastic wealth of a small percentage of America's population. They chose to display it in a dizzying array of mansions and country estates that rivaled dwellings of Europe's royalty. The same historians who attribute America's Golden Era to the Vanderbilt family suggest that they, the Rockefellers, DuPonts, Carnegies, Fricks, and Fords *were* America's royal families. This must have seemed the case to millions of Americans who did not live like Commodore Cornelius Vanderbilt and his family.

When the commodore died in 1876, trains, boats, and horses moved goods and people throughout the world. Cornelius controlled interests in railroads and shipping, and when he went to his office from his home on Fifth Avenue in New York City, a fine pair of trotters pulled his carriage. Frugal to the point of obsession, he amassed a fortune in his lifetime starting in 1810 as a 16-year-old ferry boatman in New York harbor with $100 borrowed from his mother. Shrewd and ruthless against his competitors, he parlayed his hard work into seven 200-ton steamboats by 1829. As he reached his mid-40s, he owned and operated more than a hundred steamboats and was worth several million dollars. He and his wife, Sophia, had 13 children.

The commodore was hard on his offspring and his wife, forcing her to support them from money she made from a business he gave her. While he hated trains, the Civil War showed him how railways could feed freight to his river- and ocean-going steamships. He bought up small short-haul

While not quite so elegant as George Vanderbilt's astonishing Biltmore mansion, his working stables were designed by nationally known architect Richard Howland Hunt, whose father designed the mansion. Vanderbilt's staff stored feed and bedding in the upper level where large glass windows are visible.

The aging metal roofs mimic the colors of nature in the fall leaves behind the horse barn. The horse barn housed dozens of draft animals used in farming the property.

lines. As he had done against steamship competitors, he cut prices, increased service, and steadily put the others out of business. In 1867 at age 73, he became president and owner of the New York Central. Before him, a traveler from New York City to Chicago made 17 train changes. Within two years, New York Central lines visited every city in the Northeast and ran west beyond Chicago. He had a mansion in New York City and he owned the largest steamship ever built for a private owner. When he died in 1877, he left an estate worth $105 million, and $95 million of that (about $2 billion today) went to his oldest son, William H. As Arthur T. Vanderbilt II explained in his fascinating book about his family, *Fortune's Children: The Fall of the House of Vanderbilt*, this was a time when "the finest French Chef could be hired for $100 a month . . ., a footman, carriage man, or gardener for less than $1 a day. It was a year when a successful businessman might earn as much as $10,000 a year."

William had learned from his father how to earn and manage money, yet he ignored the legacy of his father's stinginess and ill-treatment of his wife and children. By January 1883, just six years after the commodore's death,

Seen from the farm manager's back porch, the horse barn complex meandered down a gentle hillside. The upper structure held feed and bedding. Lower enclosed arms were partial stalls, while open sheds sheltered plows, harvesters, and other mechanical equipment so teams easily could hitch to them.

Vanderbilt's working horses had simple accommodations. The ceiling lights and fans are original, while heaters warm human visitors on cooler days. The floor is of paving bricks set on their sides.

his son had doubled his inheritance to $194 million and his holdings earned him $28,000 a day (about $650,000 in 2005). He had his own mansion, his own private ship, and his own private railroad car on his own railroad line. He was generous with his own children where the commodore had been frugal. William's efforts at managing his father's fortune wore him out and gave him little pleasure other than acquiring the fastest racing trotters he could find. Horses were a passion for William. He once set a track record covering a mile in 2 minutes, 15 seconds handling the reins himself. "When I lay down this heavy responsibility," he told his family, as quoted in Arthur Vanderbilt's book, "I want my sons to divide it and share the worry which it will cost to keep it." Divide it they did.

William's son, William K. or "Willie," was among the first to enjoy his father's and grandfather's success. Soon after he married, Willie and his wife, Alvah, hired Richard Morris Hunt to design a vacation home on Long Island. Hunt was the first American to complete architecture training at France's École des Beaux-Arts in Paris. His education influenced the face of American architecture for decades as he introduced, developed, and perfected a blend of classicism and grandeur that enthralled America's wealthiest families. As Arthur Vanderbilt wrote, "Richard Hunt knew his young clients very well, and he understood the function of architecture as a reflection of

The central wing of the barn held 16 large box stalls that were sometimes used for mares with young foals. Walls and stalls at the far end of the wing have been opened up to accommodate a visitors center with audio-visual displays of the farming history of the Biltmore.

Wagon tack hangs from the wall of one of the original box stalls. Below the window, the effects of a bored, rambunctious horse hoping to kick its way to freedom remain as evidence of the building's past inhabitants.

Vanderbilt advocated education for the farm staff children and provided transportation for them to a nearby school. On cold mornings, they all gathered in the blacksmith shop to keep warm. The blacksmith cared for horses' feet and repaired wagon parts.

ambition." For Alvah and Willie, after their vacation home, Hunt did a small castle reminiscent of France's Chateau de Blois for their New York City home. The country home cost $2 million, the city home was another $3 million.

Hunt designed a different kind of city home for Willie's closest friend, Oliver Belmont. Belmont was a bachelor, and Hunt's design emphasized and glorified his passion: prize racing and show horses. The entire ground floor of Belcourt Castle was a maze of stables and carriage houses. Hunt paneled Belcourt's stalls in teak, upholstered them in brocades, trimmed them in tiles, and fitted them with sterling silver harness hooks and hardware. It epitomized Hunt's guiding principle, quoted in Arthur Vanderbilt's book: "It's your client's money you're spending. If they want you to build a house upside down standing on its chimney, it's up to you to do it, and still get the best possible results."

Fifth Avenue in New York had become Millionaire's Row. Each mansion and each owner outdid his or her neighbor. These families spent $12,000 on a dinner party and as much as $200,000 on a seasonal ball lasting a single night. The generation of grandchildren of Commodore Cornelius Vanderbilt and of the Astors, DuPonts, and Rockefellers were dividing their parents' assets. It fell to the youngest of the Vanderbilt grandchildren, George, to outdo them all.

George Washington Vanderbilt was slender, with dark hair and eyes, and he was fascinated less by the family businesses than by books and literature. Three years after his father died in 1885, 26-year-old George took his mother to North Carolina to visit the Great Smoky Mountains and get away from New York's winter. The air and the view around Asheville captivated George and he decided to build a winter retreat there for his mother and himself. He bought 5,000 acres in early 1889 and construction began later that year. As the project firmed up in his mind, he wanted no close neighbors. He set out to acquire the surrounding countryside. As the estate grew, he asked for help from Frederick Law Olmsted. Olmsted was America's best-known landscape architect, having laid out New York's Central Park, the Capitol grounds in Washington D.C.; Grant and Lincoln Parks in Chicago, and university campuses for Amherst, Stanford, and Cornell.

Olmsted spent several days riding with George in a carriage over the now vast lands. Vanderbilt finally gathered 146,000 acres, nearly 228 square miles, an area roughly one-seventh the size of Rhode Island. He wanted to make a park, but Olmsted

argued against it. He said, "The woods are miserable, all the good trees having been again and again culled out and only runts left. The topography is most unsuitable for anything that can properly be called a park.

"Such land in Europe," the venerable designer continued, "would be made a forest; partly, if it belonged to a gentleman of large means, as a preserve for game, but mainly with a view to crops of timber. That would be a suitable and dignified business for you to engage in . . . . My advice would be to make a small part into which to look from your house, make a small pleasure ground and gardens, farm your river bottoms…, and make the rest a forest . . . ."

Begin at once, George said.

While Olmsted was aged and ailing, the scope of this new project enlivened him. George offered him a large staff and an unlimited budget, and Olmsted and his chief engineer, James

Gall, Jr., soon began to survey and lay out roads, gardens, trees, and a working farm to feed the hundreds of workers who swarmed across Vanderbilt's estate.

For the structures, George stuck with the family favorite Richard Morris Hunt, now nearly as aged as Olmsted. George had, as Arthur Vanderbilt wrote, "developed almost a father-and-son relationship with [Hunt] when he had helped his father work with the architect in designing the family mausoleum on Staten Island . . . .

"With this type of close working relationship, with the grand mountain site that George had selected . . ., Hunt, like Olmstead, saw the opportunity to create the masterpiece of his lifetime."

When it was completed, George invited his family to visit for Christmas 1895. His mother, his brothers and sisters, and their wives and husbands and children arrived in

Two Belgian draft horses await their first passengers of the afternoon. Visitors to the Biltmore still can tour the grounds much as George Vanderbilt and his wife, Edith, and their friends did, wrapped in warm lap robes while riding in elegant open carriages.

Vanderbilt's Carriage Barn is a much more decorative structure designed by Richard Morris Hunt, father of the horse barn designer and creator of the Biltmore mansion. Grooms and carriage drivers lived in rooms and apartments above the carriage house and stables.

At its peak, George Vanderbilt's estate encompassed 146,000 acres, which is roughly 228 square miles. The 250-room mansion covers 160,000 square feet making it the largest home in the United States. Vanderbilt farmed 1,200 acres, yielding tens of thousands of pounds of fruit, vegetables, and grain crops each year.

a chain of private railroad cars that went through Asheville and onto the private spur George had run into his property. They rode by carriages three miles up the hill through Olmsted's European forests before arriving at Hunt's 250-room chateau. It covered more than 160,000 square feet and was the largest home ever built in the United States at the time. Hunt gave it a sense of perspective in a letter to his wife, writing, "The mountains are just the right size and scale for the chateau!"

Food for that Christmas week, and for every other week, came from the 1,200-acre farm that Olmsted and his sons, John C. and Frederick, Jr., and Vanderbilt established along the banks of the French Broad River. Hunt, and later his son Richard Howland Hunt, designed and built a farm complex that included a large horse barn enclosure, a three-wing dairy barn, a creamery, and residences for grounds staff. Olmstead and George Vanderbilt planted dozens of varieties of fruit trees and vegetables, as well as grain crops. His farmers raised dairy and beef cattle. A nursery covering 300 acres sold two million young trees each year locally and by train to all parts of the country.

When construction had begun on the chateau, George had bought a nearby town called Best and renamed it Biltmore Village. Over the next several years, between 1896 and 1902, Vanderbilt added a school, hospital, church, shops, and cottages to the village. The cottages, rented to Biltmore employees, were equipped with central heating and indoor plumbing.

Hunt's horse barn housed draft horses that were used to deliver milk and farm goods to nearby Biltmore Village and Asheville. It also housed stables for farm horses that pulled implements used in field operations. In addition, the barn had a blacksmith shop, a repair shop for wagons and other farm equipment, and a large three-story barn at the rear for hay and feed storage.

George married Edith Stuyvesant Dresser in 1898, the same year that he established the Biltmore Forest School. This was America's first school for scientific forestry practices. He had developed more of a reputation as one of the country's foremost agricultural innovators than as owner of its largest home. He and Edith opened Biltmore grounds to the public on Wednesday and Saturday afternoons. He appointed directors of forestry (who had more men on payroll than the U.S. Department of Agriculture at the time), agriculture (in charge of breeding dairy and beef cattle and European hogs), and landscaping (Chauncey Beadle, a Cornell University botanist, arrived in 1890 on the heels of Olmsted and stayed on for 60 years until his death in 1950). Vanderbilt also had an estate veterinarian, a farm manager, dairy manager, and creamery manager who lived in four handsome frame houses on either side of the horse barn. Eight smaller houses for barn and dairy staff lined a road down toward the river from the horse barn.

The Vanderbilt fortune was not vast enough to accommodate the building patterns of the commodore's offspring and within five years of moving into the Biltmore, George and Edith began to conserve, reducing annual building and repair budgets from $250,000 to $70,000. Some economies did not immediately take hold. George tried to sell 120,000 acres to the U.S. Forest Preservation Commission, but it was not until after he died in 1914 that Edith partially succeeded and sold 86,700 acres at $5 per acre. Over the years while continuing active farming, she consolidated operations, reducing land holdings to 12,500 acres. She became the first woman president of the North Carolina Agricultural Society.

George Vanderbilt's passion for horses, inherited from his father and grandfather, continued on the north side of the chateau in an attached 12,000-square-foot stable and carriage house. Some 25 prize-winning trotters and lesser pedigreed riding and carriage horses lived in what is now a café. The original stalls accommodate dining tables and chairs. Today the 8,000-acre Biltmore Estate is open to the public.

The Stable Café is a clever example of adaptive re-use in architecture. Vanderbilt's 12x12 horse stalls in the carriage barn are the perfect fit for restaurant booths. Double-size foaling stalls accommodate larger groups at round or oval tables.

Shelburne Farms Horse Breeding Barn
Shelburne, Vermont

William Seward Webb's Grand Idea

Some might say that William Henry Vanderbilt saved Dr. William Seward Webb from himself. Vanderbilt certainly challenged Webb for three long years before yielding. Webb's victory was complete. He not only joined the Vanderbilt family business, he joined the family by marrying William's youngest daughter Eliza, whom family and friends called Lila.

Webb was no slouch. His grandfather, General Samuel Webb, led the Minutemen against the English at Bunker Hill. He was named for his godfather, William Henry Seward who, as Abraham Lincoln's secretary of state, was responsible for the United States acquiring Alaska. His father was firebrand editor and publisher of the New York *Courier & Enquirer*. But Webb, or Seward to his closest friends, was a physician, a less noble profession than it is today. He had studied in England and Vienna when he, at age 26, first caught Lila's eye in 1877, while he was in his residency at St. Luke's Hospital in New York City. She was just 17. They quickly fell in love.

For three years William forbade his daughter to see the older man, and long letters, routinely running 60 to 70 pages, traveled between the two. It was their only form of communication, carried by sympathetic family members. Early in his daughter's relationship with the doctor, William was concerned about Seward's prospects. He advised him to leave medicine for the stability and promise of business. Seward shrewdly followed the older man's advice and he rose through the ranks of one of the Vanderbilt subsidiaries, W. S. Worden and Company. By 1881 William relented and that December Lila and Seward married. Seward already was undertaking business trips for his father-in-law, seeking small railroads to add to the family's growing New York Central lines.

Early morning light fills the hundreds of windows of the horse breeding barn at Shelburne. Seward and Lila Webb hoped to introduce the English Hackney horse to American farming.

The massive shingle-style building came from the drawing board of New York City architect Robert Henderson Robertson, who previously had done other buildings for Webb's in-laws, the Vanderbilt family. Hundreds of large windows flood the interior with light.

More than a year before his wedding, Seward went to Rutland, Vermont, to inspect a small railway. While the business was not worth the New York Central's attention, Seward liked northeastern Vermont. Shortly before their marriage, Seward brought Lila up to visit Burlington, north of Rutland along the shores of Lake Champlain. They rented a house there through the summer of 1882. A year later they acquired 1,500 acres along the lake, and in 1883 they began construction of a comfortable, roomy home they called Oakledge. Around that time, William named Seward president (with an appropriately large salary to ensure Lila's comfort and security) of the Wagner Palace Car company of New York. This Vanderbilt-owned business manufactured sleeping cars for the New York Central in competition against George Pullman's railway and sleeping car company in Chicago. In June 1884, Seward and Lila moved into Oakledge with two-year-old daughter Frederica. By July, their second child, James Watson Webb, had joined them as well.

Recent renovations have reshingled the vast roofs and replaced broken or cracked glass panes, and even adding storm windows to former upper-level grooms quarters. The weather vane on the roof stands taller than a six-story building.

The carriage house courtyard reflects its dual use. One half remains the historic stables, in unrestored and original condition. The carriage house side of the building now is an art museum highlighting the works of local and regional artists.

William Vanderbilt died in December 1885. He left Lila a $10 million trust ($230 million in 2005) that would mature five years later on her 30th birthday. The interest, however, provided Lila and Seward the financial means to join other Vanderbilts in building their dream. For them, this was neither a mansion in New York City (although Lila inherited her father's Fifth Avenue home), nor one along the shoreline of Rhode Island. Rather, it was something more practical, hugging the shoreline of Lake Champlain, that inspired their dream. It was to be a technologically advanced agricultural operation they named Shelburne Farms.

As authors John Foreman and Robbe Pierce Stimson wrote in their 1991 book, *The Vanderbilts and the Gilded Age: Architectural Aspirations*, "Shelburne exemplified a somewhat patronizing idealism wedded to a mania for scientific modernism." Seward hoped to live full-time with Lila and their children on the farm. He planned for it not only to be a profitable enterprise but to earn enough to establish a Webb fortune and educate neighboring farmers by the example of Shelburne successes.

It was typical of centuries of experiences: Cultural realities confounded idealistic ambition. Foreman and Stimson put it plainly: "Vermonters traditionally do not complain about life's hardships; to the contrary, they endure in characteristic silence. They certainly did not welcome rich people coming up from New York and telling them how to run their farms."

For most of his life, Seward had been around horses. He was an early member of New York's prestigious Coaching Club, founded in 1875 while construction of Frederick Law Olmsted's Central Park drew to a close. On each visit to the city, he saw thousands of horses in use for commerce and pleasure. He concluded, as Foreman and Stimson reported,

that "the American horse, and particularly its Vermont variety, had descended to a very sorry state." In his own book, *Shelburne Farms Stud: English Hackneys, Harness and Saddle Horses, Ponies and Trotters*, published in 1893, he explained that indiscriminate breeding had so diluted bloodlines that no single horse breed was strong enough to pull a plow and also good looking enough to draw a carriage. In an inadvertent slap at Lila's family's business, he blamed railroads for killing long-distance coach and carriage travel which then diminished the demand for fine horses.

To remedy this situation, Seward launched a plan to introduce the English Hackney horse to Vermont and the rest of the United States. He and Lila steadily acquired another 32 farms that surrounded Oakledge. He hired New York architect Robert Henderson Robertson to design a farm barn and a horse breeding barn to get Shelburne producing its own income.

Robertson, born in 1849, two years before Seward, was a devotee of High Victorian and Romanesque architecture. Both of these styles found audiences among the very wealthy in New York City. As his reputation grew, the scope of his projects broadened and he did several stations for the Vanderbilt's New York Central Line.

Seward traveled to England and began acquiring brood mares and stallions. His ambition led Robertson to conceive a 418-foot long, 107-foot wide structure that stood free and clear of internal support pillars. Robertson held up the multitiered roof with an intricate system of turnbuckle-equipped iron rods that absorbed the outward thrust of the huge roof without transferring that lateral load onto the walls below. Seward and Lila spent $133,971 to construct the stone, wood-frame, and shingle-sided building ($3.08 million in 2005). On even the darkest days, natural light floods in through clerestory windows and dormers.

Pocket doors, including one slightly askew, served as stable doors in the large breeding barn. Webb started his Hackney horse operation with 35 mares and 4 stallions.

While Shelburne Farms uses the horse breeding barn today for farm equipment storage, in the past it has hosted cattle breeding operations, indoor polo matches, and even black-tie fundraising dinners for hundreds of guests.

A Shelburne Farms staff member props open one of several doors in the 20-stall carriage barn stables. Paving bricks, placed on their side, create the flooring. Unlike modern stables, this 115-year-old structure has adequate ventilation but poor lighting.

As early as 1896, the pressures of upholding his end of the Vanderbilt railroad business wore on Seward. He suffered nearly crippling migraine headaches. As the century drew to a close, new technologies challenged him and the railroads. Wagner Palace railway cars entered and lost a long legal battle with Pullman. The risks of failure in business and on the farm nearly overwhelmed him. His own medical training 25 years earlier was based on Civil War experiences when doctors readily prescribed morphine for many serious pains.

As Foreman and Stimson put it, Seward's "own addiction coincided with the first stirrings of social disapprobation. Once hooked, he was unable to break the habit himself. His family did not know what to do about it, either.

"Things began to unravel. By the first years of the twentieth century, his dream of breeding a perfect American horse was shattered by the rise of the internal-combustion engine. However, no attempt was made to salve the horse-breeding operation or to turn it into something else."

Shelburne Farms horse population peaked at 219 in 1891, the first year of operation. It dropped steadily over the years. In 1904, after Willie K.'s auto race, Seward and Lila sold the remaining horses and the barn saw only intermittent farming use.

The 12x14-foot box stalls housed the Webbs' carriage horses in the carriage house located near their home along Lake Champlain. One half of the carriage barn accommodated carriage and wagons, though eventually the family made room for automobiles as well.

Opening through several elegant gates onto the carriage courtyard (or at the end of this aisle to the right, out to side paths), Seward and Lila Webb's carriage horses had a comfortable stable with box stalls, double-length foaling stalls, and standing stalls along the far wall.

Seward died in 1926 and Lila followed him a decade later, leaving everything to their four children. By the start of World War II, the youngest son, Vanderbilt Webb, who had grown up and then lived with his own wife and children for a total of 45 years in the 35,000-square-foot main house, concluded it might be time to tear the place down. His offspring intervened. Son Derick began managing the farm in 1938 and by the time Vanderbilt died in 1956, Derick had made the farm profitable. In 1972, Derick's children founded Shelburne Farms Resources, Inc. (SFR) to promote sound ecological and land preservation practices. In 1983, Marilyn Webb, married to Derick's son Alec, gained family approval to convert the house to a country inn and it opened to the public in 1987. Throughout 1996 and 1997, SFR undertook a massive stabilization process on the breeding barn. The United States Department of the Interior named Shelburne Farms a National Historic Landmark on January 3, 2001. The breeding barn occasionally hosts fundraising dinners and events to benefit Shelburne Farms or other organizations. About half of the Coach Barn near the main house has become a museum of American folk art while the remainder still displays the elegance of Seward and Lila Webb's golden age of the American horse.

University of Vermont Morgan Horse Farm
Middlebury, Vermont

One Hundred Thirty Years of Breeding and Training

"This old building is the reason I've stayed here for 33 years!" With that, Steve Davis, director of the Morgan Horse Farm, shot a smile at a visitor and disappeared down the ramp to the lower level.

The old building was constructed in 1878, commissioned by a former U.S. Army Colonel Joseph Battell, and designed by a local architect/builder named Clinton G. Smith. Battell was very much taken with the Morgan horse, a breed that proved its worth repeatedly for U.S. Army cavalrymen during the Civil War. Battell, himself an avid horseman, had made it his mission in life to document the lineage of the breed. He traveled far and wide to see horses and to purchase the best stock available for a breeding program he wanted to start.

Battell traced the origin of the breed back to a foal called Figure, born in 1789 and purchased by a man named Justin Morgan who took the bay stallion to his farm in Randolph, Vermont, as a two-year-old. Historians and geneticists have argued for centuries over the breeds of Figure's parents—English thoroughbreds? Dutch warmbloods? Friesians? Whatever he was, he became Justin Morgan's horse, and after Morgan died, Figure changed hands, living out his life in Vermont and then in New Hampshire. But Justin Morgan bred Figure often and when the horse died in 1821 at the age of 32, there were dozens of the strong, compact, durable, and hardworking horses that carried on Figure's large eyes and small ears on a broad head atop a curved neck. The custom of the day was to refer to the horse in the owner's name, and, as generation after generation were born that resembled Justin Morgan's stallion, that name stuck.

U.S. Army Colonel Joseph Battell commissioned local architect Clinton G. Smith to design a barn for him to breed, raise, and train Morgan horses. Smith came up with this French Second Empire-style building, completing construction in 1878.

Through the Civil War the Morgan horses proved themselves to be dependable, easy to maintain, strong, and seemingly willing to outlast other breeds in horrible conditions. After the war, Morgans resumed duties on Midwestern and Eastern farms, pulling freight wagons and stage coaches. The market for purebred or well-bred Morgans was lucrative and Battell, after carefully determining which bloodlines were best for breeding, ordered a barn from Clinton Smith and his partner, William Allen.

Smith first appeared in building records listed as the "joiner," or carpenter for a large building in West Salisbury in 1872. Over the next several years he and his father put up a large Methodist church, renovated a national bank, and constructed a large residence in Middlebury. With William Allen, he conceived a plan for Battell's barn on his Breadloaf Stock Farm in Weybridge.

As other Smith and Allen buildings in the area demonstrate, the two architect/builders were not isolated talents following vernacular styles their fathers or other barn builders passed along to them. The French Second Empire–style building they designed and built sported a Belvedere-style cupola above the second-story hayloft. Many progressive farm journals that began circulating in the late 1800s featured architecture from around the world and one

Moonrise over the Battell Barn at UVM highlights not only Clinton Smith's stylish architecture but also the handsome statue of the Morgan progenitor, Figure, by artist Frederick Roth. The sculpture was a gift from the Morgan Horse Club in 1921 to the U.S. Government, which operated the farm from 1905 until 1951.

As part of yearling training, Jamie Charron, a horse specialist with the facility (in blue jacket, left), fits a sulky to UVM Montana, a 18-month old purebred colt. Kerry Munson and Jamie Pudims, both farm apprentices, adjust the harness tack in the arena behind the main barn.

Alfalfa hay fills the two-story loft above the ground floor of the old barn. The timber-frame post-and-beam building is joined by pegs. A high-pressure, fire-suppression sprinkler system hangs from the rafters.

of these likely influenced the designers. The decorative window trim and the elegantly carved bargeboards around the slate-covered mansard roof are more typical of an elegant urban residence of the period than a simple rural horse barn. Smith and Allen designed seven spacious stalls on the ground-floor level of the banked barn built into a gently rolling hillside. A tight horseshoe-shaped ramp at the northeast corner of the building leads down to the lower level where now another 17 stalls house foals, yearlings, and mares.

As the Golden Age dawned on America's most wealthy industrialists, they developed a taste for taller horses. Compact Morgans looked too much like the workhorses they just had given up. Trends often start among the very wealthy and filter down to people of more ordinary means. Many breeders, wanting to stay in business, diluted the lines by mating their horses with longer-legged European warmbloods. Battell, who had become the registrar for the breed, refused and he saw his short horses slipping in popularity. Despite this, he published *The Morgan Horse & Register,* a 1,000-page volume documenting performance and lineage of the breed as he knew it in 1894. Among Vermont farmers, Morgans still were popular. But by the early 1900s, with the advent of the automobile, desire for horses waned and Morgans slipped further down the wish list. By 1904 Battell began to fear for the future of the breed he had worked so hard to protect. The automobile and motor truck had become must-have items for wealthy Americans and

Keren Latimer, one of the farm's apprentices, cleans one of the main floor box stalls. UVM operates an intense 12-month unpaid internship program for as many as five post–high school students who want to learn horse breeding, training, and stable management from a hands-on perspective.

A back hallway on the first floor hides some of the tools of the barn. The structure has 7 large box stalls on the ground floor and 17 on the lower level. An inside ramp gets horses and staff from one level to the other.

Farm director Steve Davis, left, shows off UVM Montana to owner Penny Harris. Harris bought the 18-month-old colt as a yearling, which Steve and his apprentices now are training for her.

Alongside director Steve Davis' office is one of several trophy cases with dozens of first-place and reserve-finish ribbons and awards for UVM Morgans over recent years. Since 1951, University of Vermont has operated the farm, continuing its purebred Morgan program.

companies delivering in urban areas. A competing breeder to the north, Seward Webb, had completely abandoned his efforts to introduce the English Hackney horse, utterly defeated by circumstances going on around him.

Battell's Army history gave him a better chance. He had access to U.S. Department of Agriculture (USDA) officials and he offered to them, for the sum of $1, his Morgan horse breeding farm if they would guarantee to continue the breed. In 1905, the USDA took its first steps, establishing an official U.S. Morgan Horse Farm along with the University of Vermont. Two years later, it moved the operation onto his Weybridge farm.

This was the sole government field station operated for experimental work and research into horse genetics and nutrition. The farm published papers available to all horse breeders even though it performed all its research work exclusively on Morgan horses. It also successfully developed a saddle-type Morgan. Enthusiasts, breeders, and riders formed the Morgan Horse Club during the Vermont Fair in 1909 and they soon inaugurated long-distance endurance rides. They hoped to convince government farm operators that Morgans remained the best cavalry horse available. Regularly staged between 1919 and 1926, these races eventually stretched to 300 miles in length.

But gasoline- and diesel-powered vehicles were here to stay. By 1948, the U.S. Army had concluded that there was no

further application for horses in its cavalry. Some reports say that in its anxious conversion to a fully mechanized cavalry, the army destroyed every remaining Morgan horse in its protection. Even if that is true, it did not get them all. Nearly 150 animals remained at the farm in Weybridge. While the government determined what to do with the facility, it passed out stallions, foals, and pregnant broodmares to breeders and farms throughout New England. It deeded the farm and its surrounding acreage to the University of Vermont in 1951, but just 26 horses went with the barn. These animals founded the lineage that continues today.

At that point, the university named Donald Balch, a 29-year-old Ph.D. in animal breeding, as farm director. He quickly restored an aggressive breeding program using his knowledge of genetics to select fine stallions and mares. While he reestablished the quality of the Morgan horse, he also restored Battell's buildings and grounds. In 1972, he established a volunteer apprentice program that brought five to eight male and female students with strong equestrian interests to the farm for an intensive year-long education in all facets of horse farm operation and management.

Coincidentally that same year, a local graduate, Steve Davis, completed his Bachelor of Science degree in animal science. He went to work for Balch immediately as head trainer. When Balch retired in 1985, the university named Davis as his successor. Davis' family had moved from Portland, Maine, to Middlebury when he was seven, and they settled next door to Robert Baker, a very well-regarded Morgan horse trainer, to whom he

Steve Davis tries to entice UVM Montana to pose for photographs. Jamie Pudims, a farm apprentice (center), and Jamie Charron, farm horse specialist, work to get Monty to cooperate and swing his ears forward.

UVM Montana pulls Munson (right) and Charron up the long driveway to the barn. Monty, as farm staff members refer to him, after only his second time with the cart, took easily to the task following several months of training him indoors with long reins.

apprenticed himself until his graduation and appointment to the Morgan farm. Davis now oversees an annual breeding program averaging 50 mares a year for the university and private owners. From this he gets 20 to 25 foals to train and prepare for sale. The barn and outbuildings routinely house 75 to 90 animals. As the apprentice program began at the time of his arrival, he takes its students and their progress very seriously and personally. Davis never has thought of leaving.

"The challenge of this place, the animals, and the public is something that keeps me very eager every day," he explained. "I am interested in history. The aura of the New England Morgan story always holds me. The preservation of the history—and of this place—is extremely important to me."

This old building offers huge challenges for its upkeep and preservation. A recent federal grant for $365,000 provided the horses, apprentices, and the building much greater security. Senator James Jeffords sponsored legislation that matched funds from the university to install state-of-the-art sprinkler systems and a chimney liner for the building's furnace, along with other structural and safety upgrades. It's preserving hallowed ground in equestrian history.

A second photo session with UVM Montana yields better results. While Davis keeps Monty's attention, Charron brings the colt into conformation.

"The greatest pleasure I get with this barn is having someone appreciate it," Davis said. "You see people come walking up and looking at it. And they're talking in a normal tone of voice. When they step over the threshold, their voices shrink down to a whisper. It's just the aura of the place."

Ballena Vista Farms
Ramona, California

Flat Track Training in California's High Desert

Back in 1980, Don Cohn and his wife decided they wanted to establish an alternative lifestyle to what they were doing. A year earlier he had ended a busy career as a multifamily housing developer in San Diego County but promptly had started up a new business. They went looking for property, thinking five acres might give them what they wanted. Cohn, a sailor by hobby, laughed at the memory of it.

"Looking at a five-acre piece of property is like buying a sailboat. You start out looking at a 20-footer and before you know it you own a 48-foot yacht." His "yacht" was a 92-acre parcel near Ramona, California, about 60 miles east of their home. The area is called the Ballena Valley and the ranch is known as Ballena Vista, or "whale view" in Spanish. Cohn explained that originally it was a Native American name but he was wary. To this day he never has identified the hills that represent a whale's profile. But the ranch had history; it had been in the same family, the Sawdays, since 1880, though it had been fallow for decades. An aged Mrs. Sawday still lived there in a falling-down stone house. The Cohns loved the land and bid on it, hoping their price was right.

Cohn had horses when he was growing up north of San Francisco. He always wanted to get back to the animals, and his wish was granted. Cohn had friends, Bill and Shirley Tobin, whom he knew from his boating days. Tobin was a man of many capabilities with repairing boats or buildings, or in designing or constructing them. Tobin, a purist, became disillusioned by a boat business that had turned to fiberglass hulls. Cohn hired the couple to develop his land into a thoroughbred farm. Bill and Shirley took on the

Owner Don Cohn and engineer/designer Bill Tobin conceived and executed the California Mission–style adobe main barn building. The rotunda, Tobin admitted, was part of his surprise for Cohn.

Flanking the main entrance on one side is owner Don Cohn's semicircular office. On the opposite side of the entry courtyard is farm manager Manuel Ochoa's apartment. Replica Roman sculptures flank the entry gates.

Beth Pico, assistant farm manager, leads Top Approval, a yearling, down to the training riders for his morning exercise run. The 38-stall, U-shaped main barn was completed in 1992.

task of building their friend's dream. To pull a metaphor from their past lives, it was not always easy sailing. Cohn, in the midst of selling his previous business, had launched DataQuick, a real estate information technology company, and was going through a divorce. "Things were going kind of slowly," he recalled. "I was building this thing out of cash flow, along with my company at the same time."

Early in the planning, Cohn hired a well-known San Diego architect to design the first of his buildings, a crucial equipment shed and workshop. His proposal came in over budget and oversize. It literally would not have fit on the pad dimensions he was given. The experience left a bad taste with Cohn and Tobin, who agreed that they could do better.

Bill and Shirley called on dozens of horse farms in the area, talking to workers, grooms, and stable hands. They learned what worked and what didn't, and they designed Cohn's 38-stall,

U-shaped barn around a courtyard that allowed it outstanding ventilation and access.

"What kind of a theme do you want?" Tobin asked his boss. "It turned out to be adobe, like the missions, so I had to research the best way to do adobe in this day and age. To get a good insulated building, you just construct a regular building and insulate it and then put a four-inch adobe veneer around the whole thing with an air space between the adobe and the original structure so that air circulates there." Tobin's thorough investigations turned up a brickmaker whose adobe would survive the Ballena Valley climate.

Tobin saved Cohn higher building costs because, as Don recalled, "very little construction was done by professionals or subcontractors. Everything was done with our own crews with the exception of some of the major electrical work where there

Ballena Vista's training riders stretch out Roar Bucks on the outside and Top Approval as part of their morning workouts on the farm's 1/4-mile flat track. The farm started as a lay-up location but evolved into a breeding and training facility.

Beth Pico secures Arroyo Trabuco, a two-year-old thoroughbred stallion, in the Aqua-Tred water treadmill. Ballena Vista has two of these Jacuzzi-style underwater exercise apparatuses, which are very few in California.

was some danger involved. Bill hired guys who had incredible potential. Then he trained them in all the various crafts."

Cohn then acquired an adjacent property that added 130 acres. This opened other possibilities. Cohn and Tobin had decided from the start to build something that reflected California's architectural history. While none of the Spanish missions made it that far inland, land grants from the Mexican government included the one that established their new piece of property, which dated back to the 1840s and 1850s.

They finished the ranch in 1992. It had taken 12 years to build it and get it running. "And frankly," Cohn said, "it was like the *Field of Dreams*. If you build it, they will come. Well, we built it. And nobody came. For years! And I didn't know why."

Like any frustrating start-up business, the problems came from a variety of causes. In Cohn's case, his new high-desert lay-up facility arrived just as the thoroughbred horse racing

industry sank into the early 1990s recession. For another, he guessed incorrectly on some of his management personnel.

"I had the wrong people working for me here. Bill was on the construction side and he worked great. But it was the operation side that went wrong. We went through a number of managers and so-called managers." This is a story familiar to almost everyone in the equestrian industry in any capacity. "Then we found Manuel [Ochoa, his current equestrian manager] and he got this crew together. And things began to come together."

The design and plan that the Tobins devised placed two double-size foaling stalls adjacent to the manager's apartment that they equipped with large windows to watch over the stalls. Opposite the apartment, they designed an office complex including a curved workspace for Cohn. The pièce de résistance was an elegant clerestory rotunda with concealed lighting.

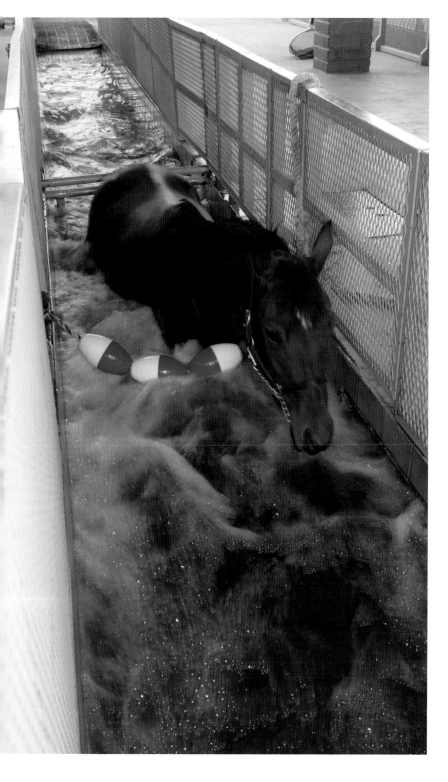

Arroyo Trabuco undergoes 20 minutes of water exercise at a fast walking pace. The 60-foot-long Aqua-Tred can take horses up to a fast trot. Water jets aim warm water at key muscles and joints.

With more than 70 horses on the property, and at times multiple sets of bridles and bits for some of the animals, the large, sunlit tack room still gets crowded. Every horse's bridle bears its wearer's name, which is a common technique on many farms.

While one of the stable staff leads Top Approval from his stall for his morning exercise session, Catch of the Century '04 looks out as if to ask when it's his turn. A skylight over each of the 10x12-foot box stalls allows daylight to fill the barn.

Farm tags remind stable hands of special feeding requirements for horses in the large outdoor individual turnouts. The name "Ballena Vista" means "Whale View," referring to whale-shaped rocks named by Native American tribes in the area centuries ago.

All the white pine paneling in the barn was milled on site from lumber harvested within miles of the farm. Owner Don Cohn asked for a rotunda for viewing horses, and Bill Tobin responded with a space fitted like a fine piece of furniture. As a surprise to Cohn, Tobin installed concealed lighting in the ceiling to make the room glow at night.

Adobe brick for the outside walls came from Encinitas, while the hand-painted interior decorative tiles came from Tecate, Mexico. The farm covers 220 acres, much of it in lush, grassy pastures.

Tobin and his onsite craftsmen finished the inside of the barn in white pine, trimmed with handpainted ceramic tiles imported from Tecate, Mexico. He knew the buildings he and his crew had constructed were solid. That didn't worry him.

"I have no idea how long that place will last," Bill explained from his retirement home in Montana, "unless they get a fire through there. I used to hold fire drills. We'd have fake fires, people would have to go to different places, pull out the hoses and turn them on. I laid out different scenarios for the places a fire could develop and what to do with the horses. Most people don't realize [that] if a barn catches fire, the horses will run back into the burning building. So you have to have a place to put them, and the only way to get them out is to put a blanket over their heads so they don't see the flames as you run them out the door. We ran through all those procedures with those guys."

Water was a great concern for Tobin as he planned the farm. He graded a hill-top and carved a large reservoir onto the property. But fire wasn't his only water worry. The farm has a pair of covered 60-foot long Aqua-Tred submerged treadmills for race horse rehabilitation. The operator can adjust their speed from a slow walk to a fast trot.

"Our Aqua-Treds are original with the property," Cohn said. "But as you stand on the deck, you realize that we have more plumbing under here than the nuclear power plant has at San Onofre, 60 miles away. Bill took what the company gave us, researched it, thought about it, and improved on it. Others have failed but ours still work. Marcelino [Gordillo, Cohn's grounds manager] learned from Bill. He has it all in his head. We have pumps and filters, and meters and heaters and gauges, and more pumps and more pumps. The water is heated, chlorinated, and then forced like a Jacuzzi around the horses. The water jets massage the horses' legs and half-float the animals."

Cohn's beautiful California mission-style buildings and Tobin's construction legacy still influence Ballena Vista's ongoing plans. The farm has become a success as a breeding, training, and lay-up facility. His two training riders run pairs of horses around the quarter-mile flat track throughout the morning. Yearlings have their first reining and saddle experiences in the round barn. The 38-stall main barn is full, as are all the outside run-in sheds and pastures. The capacity needs to grow. A dozen pregnant mares loaf in a lower pasture. Cohn has planned a "Mare Motel" with stable capacity for many more horses. "And we're going to build another stallion barn, too," he added, "all in the same style, all in the same materials. I'm not about to go poured concrete and ultramodern. That's not who we are."

Tenlane Farm—
Versailles, Kentucky

Blending Innovation with Horse Breeding

"My dad owned race horses when we were kids," Bob Evans said, "and that was our only exposure! We certainly didn't grow up in the industry. But when we got out of college, my brother Tom went directly into the business, working at the track for Woody Stephens when he was the nation's leading trainer before he died in 1998. [Stephens' horses won the Kentucky Derby twice, the Preakness once, and the Belmont Stakes five times in succession.] Then he worked for Lee Eaton in Lexington, who pretty much invented the concept of the horse sales agency in its modern form. A few years after that, Tom took off and started his own farm, Trackside Farm, here in Versailles."

Throughout this time, Bob worked in California, evolving his business into venture capital and private equity funding, with a focus on software and services companies. Over the years, he and his brother and several friends owned some horses from time to time, the 10 of them coming together under the name "Tenlane."

"It was more entertainment than anything else," Bob recalled. "Then, about seven years ago, I decided that I wanted to do this on a broader scale. Tom needed more capacity. I had sold my last business. He called me and said the property across the road was available, and if I hadn't acted, we probably weren't going to get the chance." The 300-plus-acre former cattle ranch was raw land with old cattle fencing and a small tobacco plot. Bob's original idea was to expand Tom's enterprise and resurrect the Tenlane name, but not to build a home on the farm. His business remained in California and he and wife Tracy planned to do the same while Tom managed Trackside and Tenlane.

"In this particular facility," architect Joe Martinolich explained, "there is not only the effect of light coming from outside during the day. When you see it at night, and all the lights are on, that building glows!"

Just before sunset, light streams up the valley toward the foaling barn on the highest hill at Tenlane. During fall months, long after the mares have given birth, they spend all day and night turned out in the large pastures on the farm.

The beauty and allure of horses on Kentucky blue grass proved to be irresistible, and soon Bob needed an architect for a house. He got listings from the phone book, talked to a several individuals, and asked for proposals. Before flying back to California, Bob hired Joe Martinolich of CMW Architects in Lexington to do the house. "And the house," Bob explained, "gave rise to several of the architectural elements in the barn.

"I wanted Kentucky shapes," he continued. "I didn't know exactly what that meant, but I knew it didn't mean round curvy kinds of things because you don't see that in Kentucky. I also wanted to use Kentucky materials, not rusting steel or stucco. I wanted stone and wood, materials you would traditionally find here. And I wanted something contemporary without going off to modern extremes.

"Joe put in a fourth idea, and that was the concept of surprise. As you approach the house—and this is true of the barns as well—as you enter them, move around in them, or outside of them, every time you turn a corner, there's another view that presents itself.

"He did a terrific job of pulling that off," Bob said. "To go from the front gate to the barns, you drop into the trees or you dip into a low spot. You can't see much and we isolate you, and then you come up a hill or reach a point of view and you see

horses and barns and the view. Joe dreamed up most of that: What do you see? What do you see next, as you progress from wherever you are to wherever you're going?"

"It's a little bit of a theatrical environment," Joe Martinolich explained. "You're trying to set a stage, a tone, an atmosphere. If you can do something that's interesting, but not so preposterous or full of itself, people will feel comfortable working or living in it. You frame a view, some special vista, or you arrange the way people move through a facility and see things," he said. "The way natural light works fascinates me, but even artificial light can accent materials. Light, to me, is

like a medium that doesn't just function, it has an aesthetic atmosphere to it that really changes things." Light was one of the crucial elements in Bob's and Tom's minds while they conceived the new barns.

"We had a couple principles on the barn that were different from the house," Bob explained. "We wanted to bring the outside in, meaning light and ventilation. The exterior stall doors are completely glass, and the doors and panels at the end of the barn are glass. All the stall fronts and interior stall doors are wire mesh. Joe's glue-laminated beam structure is completely clear all the way to the roof.

At first light of day, the shapes and successes of Bob and Tom Evans' foaling barn become clear. Interior air quality and light were two important factors that were addressed by the monitor roof, rows of skylights, and exterior glass doors that open onto grilled doors that let in light and air.

Morning light streams through the foaling barn by design. Big glass end doors with arched clerestory windows above and exterior glass-and-metal grille doors bring in light and air.

It's more expensive to build a structure that way because you eliminate all those less costly intermediate beams that you would normally see in a structure that size.

"Tom did the fundamental layouts of the barns. What stalls go where, where are the water hydrants, where is feed and hay stored, how do we offload straw into the barns, how do we get big trucks in and out. His business success depends on minimizing the amount of labor involved in operating the farm. I'll take credit for the way the barns look," he said, "but Tom deserves all the credit for how they work, and how they work is much more important."

"Maintenance was a really big issue," Martinolich said. "Look at the barns from about eight feet up and down. Eight

feet and down, the walls are very durable, low-maintenance, almost indestructible concrete block. These are the areas that the horses come in contact with. Eight feet and up, you've got the wood. You don't expect to see that much wood, and it has a different feel.

"Remember, it's a horse farm. Horses need plenty of fresh air and probably would rather be outside all the time. I believe that barns are there for human convenience so we can get to the horses more easily."

The exterior stall doors rarely are used for access. They are there as an exit in case of a fire for safety, but mostly they are for ventilation. The glass exterior doors are always open in nicer weather, leaving just exterior grilled doors to protect

and restrain the horses. The grilled interior doors benefit air quality but also allow a passing groom to see very quickly if a horse is down.

Martinolich's use of daylight and artificial light brought other unexpected benefits to the barns. The skylights along the roof and the fluorescent light strip that runs inside the ridgeline complement each other, and they worked out beyond the architect's expectations. Many Kentucky-style horse barns evolved from tobacco barns with tall, narrow openings for

ventilation to dry the leaves, but inside they were cave-like and dark. Martinolich understood that a Kentucky-style barn need not mimic its architectural antecedents in every way. As a result, the veterinarian and the farrier who service Tenlane enjoy working in the barns early in the mornings because they rarely need to use lights and have wide central aisles in which to work.

"In this particular facility," Martinolich explained, "there is not only the effect of light coming from outside during

It's a tranquil, almost idyllic scene and is typical of fall in Kentucky Blue grass thoroughbred horse country. Three similar but not identical barns are scattered across Tenlane's 300-plus acres, each positioned in the center of large pastures that spread across the rolling property.

An ultrawide-angle lens skews otherwise truly vertical stalls toward the dramatic ceiling. Architect Joe Martinolich specified nearly indestructible (and easily cleanable) concrete block up to 8 feet. Above that height, wood and glue-laminated wood trusses support the ceiling and roof and take the eye upward to skylights and fluorescent lights 35 feet above the floor.

Every farm has at least one kicker! Tenlane's barns are nearly kick-proof with concrete block construction up to 8 feet from the floor and strong meshed grillwork doors inside and out. Ease of maintenance was a critical concern to the owners and architect.

In each of Tenlane's barns, center aisles accommodate vehicle traffic. Skylights and grilled exterior and interior stall doors allow plenty of fresh air access and daylight into the barns on all but dark gray days.

Morning grooming takes place in natural light on most mornings in Tenlane's two yearling barns and its foaling barn. Owners Bob and Tom Evans and architect Joe Martinolich worked hard to position each structure to make best use of daylight and prevailing winds.

the day. When you see it at night, and all the lights are on, that building glows!" The fluorescent light panels along the inside of the roofline ridge cast light down onto roof panels and skylights at night by shining through the narrow monitor roof vents. The foaling barn sees most of its use in the first five months of the year, when Tenlane's broodmares will drop between 80 and 100 foals in a season. Days are short and the lights often burn through the night.

"One of the things I hoped to do with this farm," Bob continued, "was build something that would last at least one hundred years. I wanted something that had a sense of permanence to it, and hopefully it will outlast us by a long time. Horses have history. The pedigrees beget more and more history through time. I thought it might be a great legacy if a hundred years from now someone would stand here realizing that this or that great horse had come out of this barn a century before."

The farm gives Bob and Tom great satisfaction. Tom takes pride in its efficiency: There is little grass that gets mowed outside of the fences; he and his grooms waste few steps from feed to stalls and from stalls to pastures. He, Bob, and Joe measured the distances from proposed barn doors to proposed pasture gates, modifying the site plan as they went.

Inside the shadows of the barn, Tom Evans watches as his stable hands and grooms walk each yearling every day for his inspection. Tenlane's mares will produce 60 to 75 foals a year, and all of them are potential race winners.

Mares and yearlings enjoy a midday grain feed in their large pasture near one of Tenlane's yearling barns. Spacious pastures give the pairs plenty of room to forage and to run with fence gates placed in close proximity to barn doors.

"Part of what we have here is the challenge to breed successful horses, and I like the intellectual challenge of getting that done." Bob paused and watched four mares and foals directly outside his window. "But I could watch them forever. Call it beauty, whatever you want; I'll just stand around watching mares and foals playing. At the track, it's the majesty of what these animals can do.

"This sport should be dead. In a world of video games and NASCAR racing and professional football, this sport should be dead. Yet there is this connection between horses and people that you cannot describe analytically.

"Think about it," he went on. "They carry a hundred-plus-pound person and run forty miles an hour for a mile or so. That is amazing athleticism. They are marvelous creatures in terms of what they're capable of doing, and they're marvelous creatures to watch out the window.

"There are some farms where the house, the residential side of it, is separate from the horse business. But from here, from anywhere in this house, you are not more than one hundred feet from a fence. If you've come to visit us, you are going to see some horses, I guarantee you."

Hamilton Farm
Gladstone, New Jersey

United States Equestrian Foundation's Historic Headquarters

The United States Congress had established a personal income tax in 1867 to pay off national debts accumulated during the Civil War. By the end of 1872, Congress was satisfied and it repealed the tax. A depression in 1893 brought pressure on Congress to resurrect a revenue collection plan and the next year it passed a new tax on individual incomes of more than $4,000 a year ($92,000 in 2005). Numerous state and federal courts ruled for and against the tax over the next decade. The Panic of 1907 fueled an inevitable momentum toward a permanent personal income tax and a corporate tax on profits. The Supreme Court ruled that a national tax was not unconstitutional in 1911, and Congress proposed a 16th Amendment to the U.S. Constitution that gave it the "power to lay and collect taxes on incomes" in 1912. Voters ratified it in 1913. It became a political hot potato that split the Republican Party and delivered the national presidential election to Democrat Woodrow Wilson.

However, throughout the 41 years between the repeal of the first tax and the adoption of the permanent income levy, hundreds of Americans involved in establishing or enlarging businesses and essential services accumulated individual fortunes greater than some nations had held in the centuries before. Most people recognize the names of Vanderbilt, DuPont, Rockefeller, Astor, Carnegie, and others, but one name much less well-known is Anthony Nicolas Brady. Brady had fled Ireland to escape the potato famine that began in 1846. He found work as a desk clerk in Albany. By the time income tax began to make a real impact on personal wealth, Brady had become one of America's 30 wealthiest men. With substantial

In 1912, New York Financier James Cox Brady commissioned New York architect William Wiesenberger to design a farm home and horse barn on a 180-acre parcel. The result was this 54-stall, H-shaped structure with stables on the left and carriage storage on the right.

interests in railroads and tobacco, he was among the principal shareholders of New York Edison and of the Consolidated Gas Company in New York, as well as the Commonwealth-Edison Company and the People's Gas, Light, and Coke Company in Chicago. He was one of Thomas Edison's core of business partners, and sat on the boards—or chaired them—for General Motors, 2 banks, 3 rubber companies, and 13 other industries. When he died in 1912, his closest financial advisers estimated his estate at nearly $100 million. While it was just half of William Vanderbilt's, it was a vast sum.

Anthony's son, James Cox Brady, followed in his father's ambitious and industrious footsteps. Graduating from Yale University in 1904, he inherited one-sixth of his father's fortune. An avid horseman, he owned Dixiana Stud Farm in Lexington, Kentucky, named for its most successful mare, Dixie. Brady became close friends with Charles Pfizer, Jr., (eldest son of the pharmaceutical maker) through their memberships in the Essex Fox Hounds. Pfizer's passion for cross-country steeplechase riding just slightly exceeded his youngest brother Emile's interest in horses. Emile, while taking over the company from Charles, Jr., in 1905, also found time to breed horses, play polo, and race cross-country. The proximity of such equestrian enthusiasts inspired Brady to buy a 180-acre farm adjoining the Pfizer family estate in Gladstone, New Jersey. He paid just $50 per acre.

For decades, Hamilton Farm was the training headquarters of the United States Equestrian Team. Since the 1980s, the facility also has hosted events such as this multiple Pony Club competition.

This very practical design shaved the square corners off those stalls at the intersections of aisles. Cork brick floors, tile walls and ceilings, and solid brass fittings atop mahogany stalls typify this as the barn of a man passionate about his horses.

Late afternoon sunlight streaks into the main floor cross aisle. Above the stalls, ten modest dormitory rooms accommodated Brady's stable hands and grooms, and later, many Olympic hopefuls called this home as they trained for international competition.

He bestowed his wife's maiden name, Elizabeth Jane Hamilton, on the farm, and he soon hired New York architect William Wiesenberger to design a collection of elegant buildings for the place, beginning with a hunting lodge. Once Wiesenberger completed the shingle-style lodge, he and Brady added a two-and-a-half story, 65-room mansion; an athletic building; a horse barn; a bull barn; and a blacksmith shop. Tragically, Elizabeth Brady died in a railway accident in 1912, before construction of the new house or barns even had begun.

While Brady continued his vigorous work ethic, he still found time to spend at the farm. Wiesenberger's horse barn design laid out 54 square stalls measuring 12 by 12 feet. The plans specified brick construction with steel reinforcement covered in stucco. He installed unglazed terrazzo tile on the floors so horses would not slip and glazed tiles for the walls. Both materials offered ease of maintenance and cleaning.

Even the vaulted ceilings in the stables, carriage house, and the central rotunda were glazed tiles. Brady imported tall metal-tube stall hardware from England and Europe, and each corner was crowned with a 10-inch diameter brass sphere. One half of the barn held Brady's prize-winning hunters, jumpers, Hackney horses, Shetland ponies, and his Clydesdale and Percheron draft horses. The other end housed his farm wagons and his growing collection of show carriages and automobiles. Above the entry rotunda, a glass ceiling served as the floor of Brady's second-floor lounge and trophy room. It is topped with a Tiffany skylight. In his day, Brady hosted parties in this room. Dancers spun around on the glass floor, seeming to float above the rotunda below them.

On the same level with Brady's lounge, Wiesenberger incorporated 10 sleeping rooms plus attics on each wing. These were home to Brady's 25 stable hands. On the ground floor

and in the basement another 20 rooms held tack, saddles, and offices, as well as feed, grain, and hay storage. Wiesenberger also planned a 403-foot-long, 84-foot-wide sand arena behind the barn. Brady could watch his horses or his friends train and compete from the balcony outside his trophy room. Over the years he added neighboring farms and Hamilton grew to 5,000 acres. His farm manager, Fred Huyler, raised sheep, pigs, chickens, cattle, and dogs, as well as hay, oats, rye, and wheat. Huyler often showed the livestock and dogs, traveling to exhibitions and fairs in Brady's private railroad car while the animals rode in adjoining specially configured stock cars.

James Brady carried on his father's interest in automobiles, and in the early 1920s, he got involved with the Maxwell-Briscoe Motor Company that manufactured luxurious Maxwell automobiles. But the company was on shaky footing and Walter P. Chrysler took over as chairman in 1921. He merged it into his own newly formed Chrysler Corporation. Brady served on the board of both Maxwell and Chrysler. Another of his interests, Pure Oil, was a company he founded in 1923 to produce oil filters. It provided all the filters for Chrysler's earliest six-cylinder models. Over time, the filter company became known as Purolater—Pure Oil Later.

A fire destroyed Brady's main house in March 1921. He replaced it with another Wiesenberger-designed, 64-room Georgian-style brick home on the same foundation. Through the 1920s, as Brady's business activities flourished, the farm thrived. Fred Huyler kept the grounds planted with flowering plants, bushes, and unusual specimen trees. Brady died suddenly of pneumonia in 1927. He was just 48. His children, with their own lives and careers in New York City and elsewhere, sold the horses and other livestock and stopped the farming operations, even though they retained the farm. The big horse barn stayed

Brady reviewed his new horses in this rotunda and he entertained his friends in the trophy room and lounge above it with a glass floor. In his day, he hosted parties and dancers spun around on the glass floor, seeming to float above the rotunda.

(far left) Pony entrants check tack and wrap their horse's legs before competition that includes a wide variety of relay races and barrel races. An indoor ramp leads horses from this lower level to the main floor.

(left) Brady's barn plans specified brick construction with steel reinforcement covered in stucco. Builders installed glazed tiles for the walls and unglazed terrazzo tile on the floors so horses would not slip. Both materials offered ease of maintenance and cleaning. Even the vaulted ceilings in the stables, carriage house, and the central rotunda were glazed tiles.

(below) Brady imported tall metal-tube stall hardware from England and Europe, and each corner was crowned with a 10-inch-diameter brass sphere. The stables held Brady's prize-winning hunters, jumpers, Hackney horses, Shetland ponies, and his Clydesdale and Percheron draft horses.

The Glamour Girls await their events during an all-pony competition at Hamilton Farm. Architect William Wiesenberger added a 403x84-foot outdoor sand arena behind the barn.

empty for decades, interrupted by a run of duty as a hospital for injured Merchant Marines during World War II.

Through 1949, the United States Cavalry trained the horses and riders that America entered in international competition. When the U.S. Army mechanized the Cavalry in 1950, the United States was left without a team. A group of dedicated riders came together and organized the United States Equestrian Team (USET), although the group had no official home base of operations. What the team could have, now that the U.S. Cavalry no longer limited choices, was women competitors. The USET's 1952 roster included one man, Arthur McCashin, and two

women, Carol Durand and Norma Matthews. McCashin lived in the Gladstone area and knew of the Brady family and Hamilton Farm. It took several years of conversations and negotiations, but in 1961, the family invited the USET to make use of the barn and arena for a nominal fee to cover its upkeep.

Bertalan de Nemethy, head coach of the USET since 1955, began working at Hamilton in 1961 and further developed the formal training procedures in dressage and equestrian gymnastics that led to U.S. Olympic medals. Small sleeping rooms that had been home to James Brady's stable hands sometimes housed Olympic hopefuls.

At the far end of the upper floors, attics hold travel trunks and documentation of the United States Equestrian Team. The USET moved into Hamilton Farm in 1961.

On the same upper level as Brady's lounge and trophy room, Wiesenberger included 10 sleeping rooms (plus the attics) on each side. These modest accommodations were home to Brady's 25 groomsmen and carriage drivers and, in recent decades, potential Olympics competitors.

In 1978, Beneficial Management Corporation acquired the Georgian mansion house, the farm buildings, and more than 500 acres to use as its corporate headquarters. The Brady family held on to nearly 100 acres. Three years later, when de Nemethy retired as head coach, former USET member Chrystine Jones Tauber took over show jumping responsibilities. By this time, however, more competitors preferred their own training facilities and fewer came to stay at Hamilton.

Based on its continued use of and stewardship for the Hamilton barn, Beneficial Management donated the barn and 7.5 acres of the farm to the USET in 1988. In addition, the USET has use of another 200 acres on Hamilton Farm for training and competitions.

In December 2003, the United States Equestrian Team became the USET Foundation, the fundraising arm of the equestrian team's worldwide competitive efforts under the United States Equestrian Federation. Bonnie Jenkins, USEF's current executive director, points out that it is a huge task. "In 1952, the USETs annual budget was $150,000, to campaign for the entire year," she said. "In 2005, it cost $100,000 to get the team to a single overseas event in a long and geographically widespread season."

Hamilton Farm is open to the public. There is no charge for visiting the barn building; however, generous donations are appreciated.

Fork Stables
Norwood, North Carolina

Eventing, Dressage, and Environmental Protection at a Classic Timber Frame Barn

"Back as a small child, we had Tennessee walking horses," Jim Cogdell recalled. "I remember both of my brothers were into walking horses and harness horses. But as I grew older, I drifted away from horses due to my business activities and all the changes in the environmental issues that made it difficult to find a place to keep them."

Cogdell recaptured his love of horses in 1991 after he purchased a home at Brays Island Plantation, a 5,500-acre community with 60 miles of equestrian trails near Beaufort, South Carolina. He acquired some horses and kept them there.

Cogdell's focus broadened during a vacation to Western Ireland in 1997. He visited Ashford Castle in County Mayo where he took riding lessons and, as he says, "fell in love with the Irish horse." He bought his first Irish draught-thoroughbred crossbreed, or Irish sport horse, that year, and soon after he set out to learn more about the animals. He found that only 1,080 purebreds exist in the world and helped found the Irish Rare Breeds Society to help protect this breed among other native Irish animals. The horse's temperament—its intelligence, sensibility, bravery and willingness, and a strong people-orientation—when crossed with a thoroughbred, produces a horse that has more stamina and endurance than a purebred. This creates an animal more suitable to three-day eventing and cross-country types of riding and competition.

"That led to where I am: breeding two beautiful pure-blood Irish mares. Both of them have shown in the Dublin Horse Show, the Irish national show. One of them won and the other took second. That's kind

Conceived by its owner, Jim Cogdell, as a world-class equestrian center and a wildlife management open space, Fork Farm's large pond is home to migrating waterfowl, as well as serving as a large water reservoir and reflecting pool in late afternoon.

of my love: breeding them, bringing them along, imprinting them, and giving lots of quality time to them. That helped lead to Fork Stables."

Many people around Charlotte, North Carolina, know James W. Cogdell as the successful cofounder of Cogdell-Spencer Advisers, a firm known nationwide for designing, developing, and building hospitals and medical centers. He also is a patron of the arts, a conservationist, naturalist, benefactor of childrens' charities, hunter, horse breeder, and now host of the Fédération Equestre Internationale (FEI) World Cup qualifying meet. Fork Stables was the April 2006 site of this competition, one of four in the United States.

"I hoped to find a contiguous one thousand acres where I could develop my wildlife management program. I looked for a property where no roads went through it, with a river to protect boundary lines. I heard about this piece from a local congressman who knew such a property had been acquired by a trust so it would not be developed for residences or used as a dumping site. They had hoped to promote eco-tourism as one of the assets of this county. My goal was to preserve open space." Cogdell closed on the 1,300-acre property on December 28,

Stables Manager Samantha Barber rides owner Jim Cogdell's Irish sport horse Mac's Severin and assistant manager Kristen Davis works Evening Star in the lower grass ring at Fork. Some observers have suggested Fork Stables resembles a National Parks hotel from the golden era.

Samantha Barber leads the 17.2-hand Mac's Severin out of the barn before exercising him. The large wood-frame barn is 55 feet wide with 16 spacious stalls.

Fork Stables hosted one of the FEI Eventing World Cup Qualifying rounds in April 2006. The farm comprises more than 1,000 acres. Builders completed the barn in 2002.

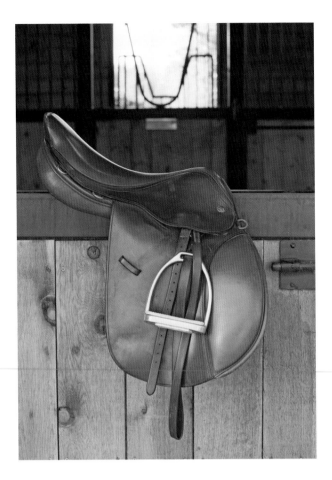

1999. One of his objectives was, along with the North Carolina Horse Council, to establish a "Mountains to the Sea" trail to enable riders to cross North Carolina on horseback. His other ambition was to host international competitions. He knew that he needed a world class barn for the latter. He contacted several equine architectural firms but concluded he preferred to work with someone closer to his property and closer to him. He went to his in-house designer, Herbie Hames.

"What I wanted was an Amish-type building," Cogdell explained. "A post-and-beam structure that would blend into the natural terrain and topography of Fork Farm. I wanted fourteen-by-fourteen-foot stalls because of my big horses, and a sixteen-foot main aisle so horses could pass each other or get tacked up in the aisle. I wanted outside stall doors so that a horse, in an emergency, could be led outside.

"I wanted good ventilation. The building is oriented so that the prevailing winds year-round would drive air through the barn and up into the monitor roof. Hot air would get sucked out. The post-and-beam idea was a touch of old country, related to the equestrian world." Hames, who had designed countless hospitals and medical centers, had not tried a horse barn before.

"This goes back a long way," Hames said, "because of our relationship. I was employed by Jim at the time. I had the opportunity to be with him when he bought the land. We walked all over it and started talking about what could be done.

Timber-frame construction, using 12x12-inch beams, some 32 feet long and each pegged to the other, fit the description owner Jim Cogdell and designer Herbie Hames envisioned for the barn. It took Mark Wray's Mill Creek Post & Beam to engineer it and make it all happen.

"One day we were standing on top of the knoll where the barn is now. 'Herbie, listen,' he said to me. 'This has to be a really first-class facility, and can we also make this a barn where I can have a black-tie supper in the main aisle'. It just came from his passion for horses, and this building developed a life of its own.

"He has a passion for design and creativity," Hames continued, speaking of his friend and now former employer. (Hames launched his own medical facilities design firm after finishing the Fork Stables project.) "Take the operations of a horse barn, but then go to the extreme of hosting a black-tie event. If you think about it, these requirements were in diametric opposition to each other. It had to be a 'cold barn' for the health and well-being of the horses. We put

alternating windows up in the clerestory and louvers across the top. Let me tell you, it's a cold barn, even in the summer when it's hot outside.

"Then Jim came back to me and said 'It needs to be dynamic.' It had to have a gourmet kitchen. He wanted to incorporate stonework into the barn. M. B. Kahn, the construction company Jim uses for a lot of his buildings, assigned a special crew to this project, and they did a lot of hand work. I recall something like seven thousand linear feet of conduit in the barn. That's because we really wanted it to look like it had been there for a long time. I remember a great question from the structural engineer. He called me up and said, 'I just want to make sure I'm reading these plans right. Is this really a barn?' " Yes, Hames replied, but one capable of

After overnight turnout, Bailey waits in his stall for morning feeding and grooming. The stalls are 14x14 feet to accommodate the large Irish draft horses and the thoroughbred crosses that yield Irish sport horses.

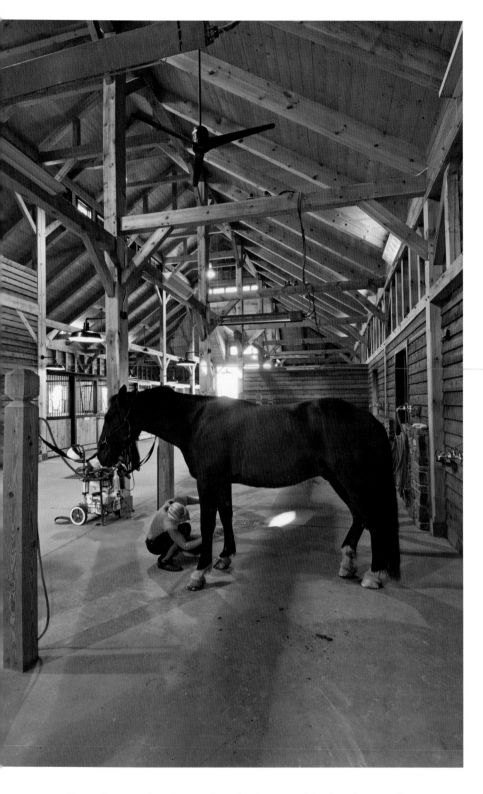

Kristen Davis tends to Evening Star's hoofs in one of the three large washing, grooming, and tacking stalls inside the barn. Dozens of dormer windows and a barn-length vented monitor roof section provide great inside light and excellent air quality.

Opposite the visitor's entrance to the barn, a comfortable lower- and upper-level lounge invites guests to enjoy the facility as much as the horses. A large deck and an upstairs balcony look out over the dressage arena and the reflecting pond below the barn.

housing 16 Irish sport horses and simultaneously hosting a sit-down dinner for 50 equestrian World Cup competitors, business associates, or family friends.

Cogdell and Hames traveled frequently and extensively during those days, primarily inspecting and reviewing the large projects Cogdell-Spencer undertook around the United States, but they also looked at barns. While they never found any specific structure they liked, Hames made sketches of ideas and various treatments.

"I built a model of the timber frame structure so Jim could comprehend what he was asking for. He fell in love with it. 'You've got it,' he said. 'This is where we're going to go with it.' We went up to the Amish area. We went up into Kentucky and talked to barn builders up there. But then we found Mark Wray."

Before Cogdell bought the Fork property near Norwood, he had looked at another site further north. Mark Wray's company, Mill Creek Post & Beam, had built several timber frame houses in a nearby community and Cogdell and Hames were impressed with his work.

"Mark cut all the timber for us and guided us through the whole engineering process," Jim Cogdell recalled. "He showed us what timber frame could do."

"The skill and craftsmanship of the people in his shop are just unparalleled," Hames added. "Our beams are twelve inches in diameter and thirty-two feet in length. Mark found the timbers and crafted the beams and posts. If you go back to my earliest conceptual drawings and follow them all the way to delivery of the trimmed timbers, Mark could structure what I had drawn. He made it feasible."

Design concepts began in 2000 and Kahn and Wray completed construction in 2002. Not only were the barn's purposes unusual, so was its construction technique. Two crews started at each end, racking in the timber frame as they worked toward the middle so it wouldn't skew out of alignment to one side or the other. When they reached the center they began hoisting the roof pieces into place. As in much older barns constructed by itinerant craftsman, oak pegs hold the 185x55-foot barn together.

In the spring of 2006, the FEI World Cup qualifying events were held at Fork Stables, over a challenging course designed for Cogdell by Captain Mark Phillips, a British Equestrian Team 1972 gold medalist who now serves as Chef d'Equipe of the United States Equestrian Team's three-day eventing team. Local and regional newspapers and media praised the international competition, the facilities, and Fork's natural beauty an hour outside of Charlotte. More than 4,000 spectators attended.

"We worked until after midnight each night," Cogdell recalled, "and usually we started again at four-thirty the next morning to get ready for the World Cup. We irrigated all the cross-country course so the footing would be proper for

The tack room displays a few of the owner's hunting trophies and a handful of his horses' show and competition ribbons. The opposite end of the room is a gourmet kitchen for staff midday meals or for banquets for dozens of guests often in formal evening attire.

Jim Cogdell fell in love with Irish draft horses in 1997 on a trip to Ireland, where he took lessons on one. He now breeds and trains purebreds and thoroughbred-crosses called Irish sport horses. He is a cofounder of the Irish Rare Breeds Society to protect the breed.

riders under the pressure of galloping at six hundred meters per minute.

"This was Jim's passion," Hames explained, "his love of horses, his love of entertaining, his love of creative architecture. Yet overriding each of these is his love of the environment."

"Most everybody who came as spectators," Cogdell continued, "did *not* understand the level of eventing and the discipline of these horses and riders they were watching. They wonder what this sport is about, especially when they see riders dressed in such formal attire, so the best way to educate them is to teach them about open land.

"I'll be sixty-five in June," he explained. "The property here at Fork will be left in a support organization for education about wildlife habitat, foraging management, soil conservation, and children's education. That's kind of the bottom line of the farm."

As owner Jim Cogdell and designer Herbie Hames conceived the barn, the goal was for a structure that was timeless in appearance. The barn stretches 185 feet across the knoll above the outdoor dressage arena.

Heronwood Farms
Upperville, Virginia

This Horse Barn Redefined the Horse Barn

Robert Smith had an idea, "a life-style modification," he called it. It was 1982 and Smith was an overly hard-working East Coast real estate developer and builder. He was born and raised in Brooklyn, New York, and had spent the Sundays of his youth with his family visiting an uncle who operated a farm in White Plains. "We always had a great family time there," he recalled. He proposed to his wife finding a place about 90 minutes from their home in Maryland where they and their children could do the same.

"But what are we going to do out there?" his wife Clarice asked him. "Once you get there and see the flowers and trees and grass and the pond and you go fishing…, what are you going to do if you plan to go out there every weekend?"

"I'm going to breed and raise horses!" he said.

"What do you know about breeding and raising horses?" she asked.

"Nothing," he said, "but I'm a quick case learner!"

They began a search for their dream property that consisted of 200 acres. Within a year, Smith had joined with close friends to buy 10 horses in England to race there. They hired three separate trainers, had a lot of fun, and won some events. "Prior to that," he recalled, "I had *no* experience, none at all, in riding, in racing, in any aspect of horses. It was just this time of the ten horses in England with these friends having a good time . . . ." With his interest intensified, he refined his plan.

"The place we looked for *had* to be of such physical attributes that we would want to go there each weekend," he explained. "Because once you own a place in the country, you build in a certain responsibility. I wanted

Owner Robert Smith asked his architects for a "version of an early nineteenth-century Virginia barn, but I wanted the barns to be more contemporary in terms of glass, in terms of ventilation, in terms of all the things that we know are very good for horses."

By any standards, even those of a late winter day of melting snow, Heronwood is a beautiful farm. Landscape architect Morgan Wheelock placed barns, paddocks, roads, and walkways to treat the eye to lovely vistas.

us to be drawn to a place where the activities, the lifestyle, would be a Mecca every weekend."

After another year of looking, he and Clarice acquired a 50-acre parcel from businessman/entrepreneur/sports team owner Jack Kent Cooke. They added two neighboring pieces of land that took their 200-acre ambition up to a 580-acre reality called Heronwood Farm in Upperville, Virginia. At that point, it was time to build their Mecca.

Smith learned about a landscape architect/land planner named Morgan Wheelock in Boston who had designed horse farms. Smith invited him to see the property. The two men hit it off, Smith liking in particular that Wheelock was "sensitive to the contours of the land and wanted to do everything in the most naturalistic, aesthetically pleasing way." Wheelock promptly began to plan the farm, siting the buildings and laying out the roads, pastures, and fences. He

had theories about placing buildings in the landscape, using natural ventilation and natural light, and designing buildings that were healthy and safe for horses. But Wheelock was not a building architect, and while Smith knew dozens of architects as a developer and builder, he knew no one who did horse barns. Smith wanted a "contemporized version of an early nineteenth-century Virginia barn, but I wanted the barns to be more contemporary in terms of glass, in terms of ventilation, in terms of all the things that we know are very good for horses," he recalled.

Robbie Smith and John Blackburn were two architects who met while working at a large firm in Washington, D.C. They became friends and while their early careers separated them geographically, they maintained a friendship that eventually led them into business together back in D.C. Robbie lived in Middleburg, the nearest town to Upperville. He got a call from a

The prevalent architectural form in northern Virginia is Federal style. Architects John Blackburn and Robbie Smith repeated its characteristic elements along the windows and dormers.

Neither Robbie Smith nor John Blackburn had designed a horse barn before this one, but landscape architect Morgan Wheelock had collaborated on several. Wheelock taught the building designers the importance of good natural lighting and excellent interior ventilation. The ridge row of skylights provides abundant light even on gray days.

friend of Wheelock's who told him the Boston designer needed an architect to do a horse farm in Upperville. Did Robbie know anyone who might be interested? It took him just seconds to say, "Sure. Us!"

Then, as John Blackburn recalled, "We thought, 'Oh my God, what do we show him?' We knew they were interviewing other architects, but nobody we knew was doing horse farms. We found out they wanted buildings that fit into the natural environment. So Robbie, being from that area, photographed barns, houses, sheds, commercial buildings, everything we could think of in the area that fit into the natural environment.

"As far as we could tell, not a single building we photographed was designed by an architect. Most of them were done in the last century and the previous century. They were all types of buildings in all types of conditions with all kinds of design quality. We projected the pictures onto the wall of our studio, put paper up, and drew over them, sketching them.

"They were vernacular, organic if you will. They were built from local, naturally-found materials. They were Federal-style forms, which repeat themselves." They took their sketches to their presentation, announcing that if the Smiths wanted buildings that fit into Middleburg, these were the forms, shapes, and materials that they needed to use.

Crocket, a Dutch Warmblood/ thoroughbred cross, looks out of his stall awaiting his morning feed. The stalls, laid out in symmetrical balance, open onto the center aisle.

When Robert hired Smith and Blackburn, he took them and Wheelock to inspect prominent thoroughbred farms in Lexington, Kentucky. "We talked to guys like Will Farish at Lane's End Farm, Sheik Maktoum bin Rashid Al Maktoum, and Seth Hancock, and to their farm managers," he explained. "We wanted to find out if they were building new barns today, based on the experience that they had, what would they *not* do, what would they do differently, and how would they improve what they had?" This information, along with Wheelock's suggestions, helped Robbie and John start designing a broodmare/foaling barn and a yearling barn for Heronwood.

"It has the Federal shape," John Blackburn explained. "That also is functional. The Federal shape forms pockets for the

doors. The doors slide into the wall. Instead of covering the wall, we used the shapes, the elements of the Federal style to accommodate the large doors. And we repeated that shape over and over along the windows and dormers.

"There's another element—psychology. It's psychology that makes you use nicer materials where you're trying to create a feeling. The broodmare barn entrance is at the cross aisle. There is a stone terrace. Inside, there is nicer reception room than in the yearling barn. You approach it from the side because you're bringing a client there who is interested in breeding. You want to make your sales pitch, talk about your blood lines, your history.

"With the yearling barn, you approach it from the end because they're bringing you the yearling. You're not there to

From the start of their horse barn design career, John Blackburn and Robbie Smith emphasized health and safety of the horse above all considerations. Heavy mesh steel doors allow stable staff to see if a horse is ailing, and the lock peg, which stores in a matching brass receiver on the low wall near it, never will catch on a horse and tear its skin or a muscle.

After a gentle exercise ride in the snow and a thorough grooming, Berkeley Gunnell blankets Theodore, a 9-year-old Shire/thoroughbred cross. Gunnell leases the Yearling Barn from Heronwood and operates her own business, Greyledge Stables, boarding and training horses for a number of clients.

An array of bridles and bits hang in the tack room in the middle of the barn. Blackburn's design places human resources at the center of the 16-stall barn to minimize steps for chores.

study blood lines, you're there to buy and you want to see that yearling walk. That's why we put the circular driveway on that end," Blackburn explained. "It's a theory Morgan Wheelock gave me in my early training years that has some sense. It's in the thoroughbreds where you're selling the horse." Breeding and raising horses and selling them became Robert Smith's avocation once the builders completed the barns at Heronwood.

"I wanted to do a first-class operation," Smith recalled, "because what I had in mind was to buy, over time, twenty high-class mares and breed them to the best of the best. I bred to Nijinsky, I bred to Storm Cat, to Seattle Slew, to Alydar, to Mr. Prospector. You name it. Of course, even when you breed to the best, you never know what's going to come out. But at least you have a better chance. And we did very well. We sold at Lexington, at Saratoga, at New Market [in England], at Deauville [France]."

During its years as an active breeding farm, Heronwood dropped 16 to 18 foals a year. Smith would sell 12 to 14 of those, keeping the others to train and race under his colors. "We sold more than two hundred horses. But after more than fifteen years in the business, I felt I had done everything I had wanted to do.

"And the breeding fees, the stud fees, just were getting out of hand. To breed to Storm Cat was five-hundred-thousand dollars. I didn't want to have that much money tied up in horses. At different stages of one's life, sometimes you transfer priorities, your interests."

But Heronwood was nowhere near its twilight. The farm boards 120 polo ponies during the summers. These horses come from Florida to rest through the fall and winter. A local trainer leases the yearling barn for her clients. Robert and Clarice Smith also have 55 alpacas that they breed, show, sell, and shear for their fiber.

In addition, the farm is the site of the Upperville Colt & Horse Show. This is the oldest horse show in the United States. Every year since 1853 (including Civil War years), the horse show has taken place on this property during the first week of June. In any given year, 1,200 horses and riders and 30,000 spectators watch pony shows, hunter-jumper competitions, and side-saddle and jumping events under 200-year-old oak trees.

Heronwood was the first horse barn complex John Blackburn and Robbie Smith designed. Blackburn continues to this day out of offices in D.C. where horse barn architecture comprises a large percentage of his work. In the 22 years since then, he has seen barn design improve.

"The biggest change from my perspective was Morgan Wheelock and his influence on me and his concepts. Where he got them, I don't know. If he discovered them in the middle of the night, I don't know. My relationship with him was the focus of my growing career.

"For example: transmission of disease. His theory was that you put the building perpendicular to the prevailing breeze so it ventilates vertically. The horse that is transmitting disease

With a snowstorm just past, Berkeley Gunnell enjoys an easy ride on Theodore around the alleyways between pastures. After owner Robert Smith retired from active thoroughbred breeding and training, he offered his yearling barn to Gunnell for her independent boarding and training operation.

won't give it to the next horse because it's going up and out of the barn. People used to say that you just open those big end barn doors and the wind will blow right through. That may or may not happen. But nothing is there to facilitate the wind. And if you do get wind and you have a virus in the barn, it will go from one horse to the next."

Wheelock's and Blackburn's theories of health and safety came out of the thoroughbred industry in which they worked. In the early days, a rule of thumb dictated that the foal was worth as much as the barn.

"If you are spending five-hundred-thousand or a million dollars on a horse," Blackburn continued, "you better be thinking about your barn. And it may take another million dollars to create an environment that will protect your horse.

"Most of the market is not interested in what we do. Some people are. Many farms today are nice barns for nice horses. But other owners have a sense of design, aesthetics, and finish, and how things are done."

"Certainly," Robert Smith concluded, "during the time that I was involved with horses, these barns worked very well for me, in terms of cleanliness, maintenance, health of the horses, and their aesthetics. It's a beautiful place with rolling land and attractive buildings that were built to very high standards of design. I've tried to maintain the entire farm at the highest level, and it's become our Shangri-La."

Barn manager Kristine Kelly leads Crocket from his snowy pasture back to the barn for morning feed. Landscape architect Morgan Wheelock planned all the paddocks and alleys between them, as well as the roads and barn placement.

During its years as an active breeding facility, Heronwood Farm dropped 16 to 18 foals a year. Smith would sell 12 to 14 of those, keeping the others to train and race under his colors. He sold more than 200 horses.

Stoneleigh Farm
Middleburg, Virginia

The "Cathedral for Horses" provides Olympian Joe Fargis with year-round facilities for teaching and training.

When Mary B. Schwab was growing up in California, her sister had horses. Mary B., as everyone who knows her calls her, remembers going along on Western trail rides. Her parents owned a couple of race horses over the years, and she recalls going to the track, but that really never was part of her life. Her career kept her mostly indoors in an office. But in the early 1980s, riding beckoned to her again. She went with a friend to a dude ranch and began taking riding lessons soon after that.

Her first horse was a quarter-horse named Jeremy, now 30-something and retired. Several years later, in early 1995, she bought a horse for a talented amateur rider (coincidentally also her veterinarian) who had trained with U.S. Olympic 1984 gold medalists Joe Fargis and Conrad Homfeld. Joe and Conrad had formed a business together in 1978, Sandron, that served the show-jumping industry. After Mary B. and her rider amicably parted company, she took Jeremy and the competition horse to Joe. Although he didn't show the horses himself, Joe got riders to compete with them. Under his guidance, she bought another horse, and then they began buying horses together regularly. All this happened while Mary B. lived in Atlanta, and Joe, who was born in Virginia but had been away for years and spent months on the road training, teaching, and competing, was interested in getting back home.

"We started coming to the Upperville Colt & Horse Show and just hanging around here," Mary B. recalled. "During the beginning of June when the show happens, it's really pretty here. I fell in love with the

Modeled after a Sears Roebuck kit barn from the 1920s she saw in a barn history book, farm owner Mary B. Schwab commissioned architect Peter Block to update the design as an indoor arena. Sliding windows provide excellent ventilation.

countryside." She had looked at properties in Florida to be close to the winter horse show season, and she considered Long Island but disliked the idea of trucking horses across Manhattan to and from most shows. In 1998, she started seriously looking for land in Virginia. Following months of discouragement one of her friends called to tell her about another friend of a friend who needed to sell her farm. Mary B. looked at it on a Friday, Joe saw it Sunday after a show ended, and they bought the place with the goal of establishing a high-quality training and boarding farm for students and their horses to gain the skills needed for upper-level show jumping. An architect friend from Atlanta, Peter Block, developed plans to remodel Joe's house, followed by Mary B.'s main house the next year.

"But the first thing we did," Mary B. explained, "was build the second barn. I asked Joe how many stalls we should look for," she laughed. " 'Whatever size it is, it will get filled,' he said."

"This barn is brand new," Joe explained, walking through a nearly identical barn joined to the older one. "When we came here in 1998, there was an apartment and twelve stalls here. We duplicated this piece over there. Where we have wash stalls and cleaning stalls now, there were boarding stalls. The feed room now is the tack room. The former tack room now is the feed room. This barn was very simple: laundry room, tack room, bathroom. We tried to keep it as simple as possible, that was my only rule." Over his career, Fargis had seen dozens, if not hundreds, of barns. Experiences and observations doubtlessly

After considering property in Georgia, Florida, and Long Island, New York, Mary B. Schwab fell in love with northern Virginia while attending horse shows with her business partner, Olympic equestrian gold medal–winner Joe Fargis.

Soon after acquiring the farm, Schwab and Fargis expanded its barns, doubling their size by duplicating an existing structure and connecting the two with a cross aisle. Turnure Architecture & Design in Middlebury made the plans from Fargis' specifications and requirements.

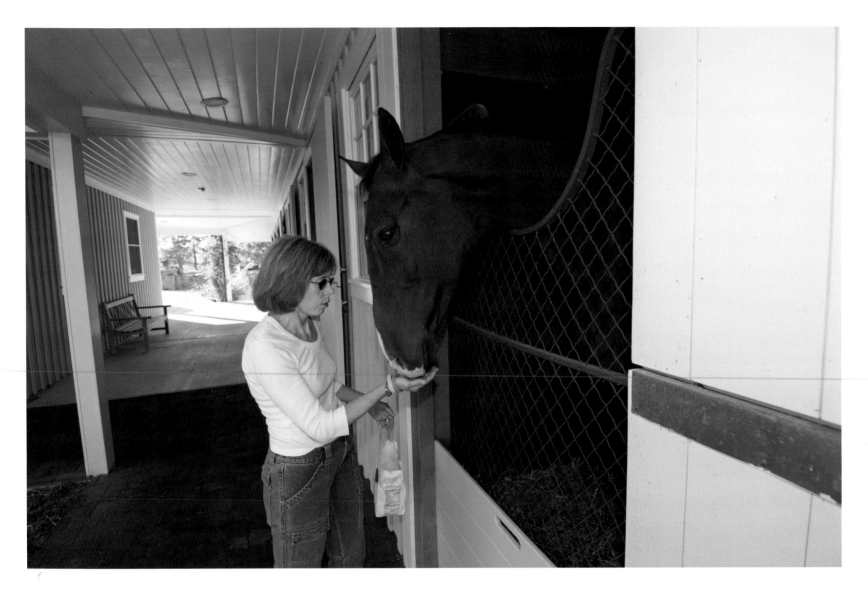

For Mary B. Schwab, the best part of her day is late afternoons after her stable staff has finished. She slips down to her barns with a bag of treats for all the horses. Horses have brought her the beauty of this farm, she says.

clarified in his mind what he would do when the chance came to define his own.

"I'm not an architect, but these are twelve-by-twelve stalls and we duplicated that original barn. All the bits and pieces reflect my taste. I hate things in the aisles, so all the hoses are recessed. I hate wheelbarrows and pitchforks in the aisles, so they all go in a little house along the aisle. The horses can't look into the center aisle, it keeps it cleaner looking, but they can look outside, so it's not claustrophobic for them. It's quite easy to load and unload horses here because the driveway goes all the way around the barns. It didn't used to do that." The matching barns form an H-shaped complex.

"I love it," Mary B. said. "And I'm glad that people get to enjoy this place, to enjoy the natural beauty and this facility, mainly through Joe. But the indoor arena was totally my plan in that I didn't want it to look like an indoor arena!

"There are much bigger ones, but mine is prettier. The average arena looks like a warehouse from the outside. They have to be tall because they are big. Joe, my architect Peter Block, and I went and looked at a lot of arenas. Peter is not a horse person. But he started doing research and he found a picture in a book of a barn that was actually sold as a Sears & Roebuck catalog kit that came in pieces in the 1920s. There is one down in Orange, Virginia."

Architect Peter Block remembered her assignment vividly. "Mary B. told me she didn't want this arena to look like anybody else's around there," he recalled. "'I want it to feel like the rest of this farm,' she said, 'as opposed to being just a utilitarian structure that sometimes these buildings can be.' Joe gave me the dimensions he wanted for the arena.

"We predominantly do historically-based architecture, so we have built a fantastic library. With this horse assignment,

we did the same thing. I went and got every book that I could, new and old. One of the books I found was *The American Barn*. In it, I saw the Sears kit building called the Sylvania that was a Belmont Barn. A Belmont is one in which there are stalls in the interior and a track that is still enclosed surrounding those stalls. That's so, in inclement weather, grooms can still walk the horses."

Mary B., Joe, and Peter went to Orange to meet the owner, Helen Marie Taylor, and see her barn. "We visited her. She has such a great attitude about life," Mary B. said. "We loved the barn's shape and what it looked like from a distance. Peter took that and started his work." Block's work was not without several serious challenges, however.

"This Sears kit building that I thought was extraordinarily beautiful," Peter remembered, "gave us one challenge, which was how to do a building that is much wider and has nothing in the interior so it has to be a clear span. We came up with the idea of the glue-laminated scissor trusses to accomplish that reach.

"One of the beautiful things about the barn in Orange was its wraparound glass. How do we do that? Our idea was to use three large barn sashes and have hardware and tracks so that you can slide two windows open and they'll stack in each bay. This gives it the ability to feel much more like a covered ring when weather permits as opposed to an indoor ring when the weather is inclement."

One substantial challenge was to site the arena. Stoneleigh Farm, by anyone's description, is beautiful, with rolling hills, century-old stone walls, and lush tree stands surrounding the property. The twin barns, with their low, gentle gables, completed by Turnure Architecture & Design in Middleburg, fit Mary B.'s sensibilities perfectly while meeting Joe's specific

Fargis has strong feelings about clutter in barn aisleways. That includes horses' heads. While horses can see each other through door and wall grilles, exterior doors open in such a way to allow the horses to look out and see their barn mates.

The corner of Fargis' office is orderly, tidy, and organized, like the rest of the barn and all the property. Schwab and Fargis took over the farm in 1998.

(opposite page) The one exception to horse heads peeking in the center aisle is the miniature horse, Pirate. Fargis' discipline keeps the barn tidy except when Pirate kicks its bedding through the gate.

Glue-laminated scissor trusses support the arena completed in 2000. The regulation dressage arena is rimmed with horse blankets that Schwab's and Fargis' horses have won in numerous competitions.

An assortment of saddles lines the wall in Fargis' office facing his desk. From his office door he can see three of the barn's five aisles and quickly determine if everything is all right or anything is wrong.

horse care and safety requirements. Yet, even an elegant arena that honored and improved on an 80-year old design was going to be large.

"Joe and I worked for months on where to put it because I didn't want to look down and see this monster building! Then Peter found the spot!"

"Not all the credit for the arena's location is due to me," Peter explained. "We wanted it where you didn't have to take the horses too far, but not so close that it looked large. By putting it down in that valley, it did make it more discrete from the road. The landscape architect, Ed Daugherty from Atlanta helped in the siting. It was very much Ed, Mary B., Joe, and us thinking of how this thing works, how it looks, and how it fits with the farm. There was a lot of discussion about pulling all that together.

"There was an interior designer, Billy Baldwin, whose whole concept was suitability. To him, that meant doing something that not only works well, but that lasts, that continues to work well. Mary B.'s idea of having the arena be part of Stoneleigh Farm was that same concept. It's not an alien structure. It fits in with everything else that is there. And you can't really tell when it was built. Her main house, I believe, was built in 1832. We completed the arena in 2000."

"When we were building it," Mary B. recalled, "there is one road, County 611, that comes right at it. I got questions from friends. 'What are you building over there?' 'It's the Cathedral of Saint Joe,'" she told them to startle them and make them laugh at her reference to her friend and equestrian manager, Joe Fargis.

On a wagon along one of the farm roads, dozens of jump cross rails await the next event. The stacked stone wall in the background is typical of those found in this region of northern Virginia.

"It's such a pretty building; people are always surprised to see it." For Joe, the building is very suitable, offering protection from the summer sun and effectively catching prevailing breezes. "It's as much as twenty degrees cooler inside here on a summer day," he said. "It's just a wonderful place to work."

"Horses have brought me the beauty of this place," Mary B. continued. "I enjoy the animals themselves. I enjoy watching them show, of course, but the best part of my day is in the afternoon after the grooms are gone. Then I go down to the barns and give every horse a treat. I enjoy being around the animals. They bring such a calm peacefulness to life that you just don't get from other things."

Following a lesson in the indoor arena, one of Fargis' students makes her way up to the barn. The small building at left is storage for show and competition gear and trunks.

Culver Academics
Culver, Indiana

Equestrian Education in an Exceptional School

"We believe that the horses are one of the best tools there are for teaching leadership," Ed Davis said from his office inside the Castle, Culver Academies' legendary equestrian facility. "Most of the boys that come in, and many of our girls too, have never ridden a horse before, or they have only limited experience. These kids start as young high school students, ninth grade and up. If they can develop the confidence to work around a thousand-, fifteen-hundred-pound animal, to groom it, pick up its feet and clean them, saddle it, and put a bridle on it—and that means putting their hand in its mouth—and then getting on it and getting it to do what they want it to do . . . this is the nucleus in the development of leadership."

Culver Academies is all about leadership. The school's website and its printed materials emphasize the knowledge, skills, and education that students receive there, all directed toward leadership in further education and career. A segment titled "Why Culver?" recounts the memories of dozens of CEOs, directors, company founders, judges, and professors who make it clear what the school did for them. One graduate, Kenneth Ackerman, wrote that "as a teenager, I learned that you get things done by leading people, not by driving them."

Culver Academies now comprise two schools. Boys attend Culver Military Academy. Students who ride in the equestrian program are members of the Cavalry Unit, the 75-member Black Horse Troop. The honor organization within the troop is called the Lancer Platoon. While the Black Horse Troop does drills and parades on Sundays (and has participated in more than a dozen presidential inaugural parades), the

The 88-year-old "Castle" is one of the landmark buildings at this prestigious boarding academy. Grandstand seating along the hillside accommodates visitors who watch weekend and holiday drills by the legendary Black Horse Troop and the Equestriennes.

Lancers perform complicated routines accompanied by the live band. They appear at the big weekend events including alumni weekend, parents weekend, and graduation. For girls in Culver Academy, their honor equestrian organization is called the Equestriennes. They perform on the same major weekends as the Lancers, though at different times. About 40 of the 300 young women on campus participate in the women's troop.

"The Troopers and Equestriennes work extremely hard," Davis explained. "When they have equine science classes, they ride as well as take classroom lessons. They run back to their barracks, change clothes, run over here, groom, saddle, and bridle their horse, and do their lesson. After the riding session they bathe their horse, clean and store their tack, run back to the barracks, shower and change clothes, and then go to their next academic class."

Everyone involved with the horsemanship department takes equine science classes twice a week during their first and second years, and then once a week during their third and fourth years. This regimen helps students develop a work ethic. They come to understand the time commitment required to deal with the horses and also do a good job with everything else they undertake at Culver.

The education is complete. Men and women students learn how to play polo, how to jump, and how to execute dressage routines. They learn formal riding, how to participate in horse shows, and how to set jumps for those shows. They learn how to age a horse by its teeth and how to identify illnesses and noncommunicable diseases that are caused by lack of attention from their human caretakers. By the time they finish the program, they can prepare a horse for a veterinary visit by taking its pulse and respiratory rates. Ed Davis and his instructors teach and test their students on all these topics and skills.

"Anybody who is going to continue as a polo player or a jumper or just take recreational rides on trails needs to know these things," Ed said. "It just makes better horsemen out of them. It's much more humane for any of them who do decide to own a horse that they have the skills to care for one the way it should be cared for."

All this takes place in and around the 88-year-old Castle, a massive red brick building with turrets and crenellated battlements. The riding hall was designed to resemble European cavalry stables. At one time it was one of the largest in the world and the biggest in the United States. It easily will accommodate arena polo, as well as military exhibitions and drill demonstrations. Once winter settles into northern Indiana, all the classes move into the building. Davis also prefers putting new students on horses for their first time within the contained boundaries of the arena.

"It is the stabling that is a bit outdated," he continued. "We have stabling for 120 horses, and for the program to have the

The name of the architect of this grand edifice is lost to history. But hundreds of Academy men and women students have learned horsemanship, dressage, jumping, and polo, as well as self-confidence and leadership skills, inside this building.

A copy of *The Cavalry Journal*, a quarterly publication from the U.S. Cavalry Association, lies open in the lounge of the Castle. Pages 242 and 243 record the 1923 training maneuvers of the Third Cavalry from Fort Myer, Virginia, and the Fourth Cavalry from Fort McIntosh, Texas.

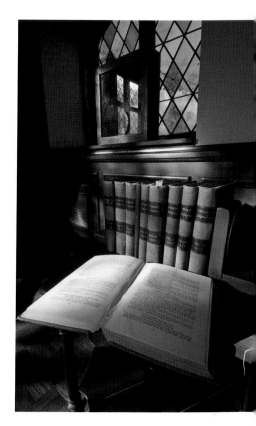

Standing stalls, all 120 of them, are numbered with corresponding grooming brushes for each horse. Near-term plans by architect John Blackburn call for replacing these with 100 10x12-foot boxes by expanding the building through two large turnouts to the north.

Despite criticism that standing stalls are narrow, students find adequate room to groom and tack up their horses. The new boxes are intended to appeal to potential donors accustomed to seeing their own horses in more spacious accommodations.

number of horses that we have, tie stalls, or standing stalls, four feet in width, are the most efficient. There is enough room for the horse to lie down and get up. But it's just so important that the horses get out and not just stand in there for an entire day and night.

"They have to be turned out or exercised. That's a big part of the health of the horse. It's a giant puzzle for us to make sure that all the horses get utilized in different activities throughout the week. And when they're not being used, we have to make certain that they get out into the paddocks for some exercise. It takes a great staff to make that work out."

The school has plans to simplify that puzzle. It has hired John Blackburn, of Blackburn Architects in Washington, D.C., to plan and design a major expansion that begins in April 2007. They have come up with a phased plan that is as ambitious in scope as it is beneficial to students, faculty, the school, and potential donors.

Initially, Blackburn's crews will rebuild the stables, turning 120 standing stalls into 100 10x12 boxes. North of the stables are two large turnout areas, and beyond them is the old armory where equine science classes take place and where fixed practice horses give polo players training at hitting the ball with the mallet.

"The armory will become the entrance building," John explained, "with classrooms that look over into the arena. The arena will take an L-shape. The two center turnouts will move

Several identical tack rooms, plus one specifically for polo gear, house the gear for dozens of young men and women riders. By the time students finish the program they can age a horse by its teeth, identify illnesses and noncommunicable diseases that are caused by lack of attention from their human caretakers, and prepare a horse for a veterinary visit by taking its pulse and respiratory rates.

to the east where tennis courts are located now, and that new enclosure will accommodate the new box stalls."

Blackburn's plans link all the buildings with interior passages for safety, as well as comfort. Leading a horse from one building to another over January ice puts both horse and student at risk. The existing riding hall will have new sideboards, better lighting, new windows, a much nicer footing, a new watering system, and an elevator to provide handicapped access to the upstairs seating.

At first, jumping training is performed at a walk with an instructor leading students through a course. This not only leads horse and rider to a jump, but it forces the rider to maneuver and control the horse as well.

"The third phase," Blackburn continued, "will include a new 100-by-200-foot indoor arena. It's not as long but it is wider than the other hall and closer to regulation sizes for dressage and hunter-jumper meets. Where Culver used to be all male [until 1971], now it is more and more female, perhaps half and half, and they are working to add more sports that young women riders are interested in. They have coeducational polo, as well as separate men's and women's teams.

"The new structures will look like the Castle, in a way. We're being sympathetic to that architecture, but we will not replicate it. One reason is for costs. The other reason is that it's not honest architecture to do that. We'll use red bricks; it will have some battlements in some of the areas where you can make a visual connection between the new and old buildings. But I'm not going to make it look like a fortress; you want to be able to look at a building and say, 'Ah, that's the arena, it's not an arena made to look like a classroom building,' which is what the original riding hall was designed to look like."

While new classrooms, elevators, riding surfaces, and windows will benefit the students, it is the new stables that will have the greatest impact on the health and well-being of the horses. It also will address concerns that several potential donors have expressed about offering valuable horses to live in cramped standing stalls.

The large indoor arena easily accommodates indoor polo. Both men's and women's polo teams practice together. For decades, this was the largest indoor arena in the United States.

Horsemanship Director Ed Davis is a former professional polo player. In 1990, after retiring and returning to school to earn a teaching credential, Culver called on him to teach and coach the game to its students.

Equestrian architect John Blackburn has completed plans that will convert Culver's 120 standing stalls to 100 box stalls by moving the building out to engulf these two large turnouts behind the Castle. Additional turnouts will replace existing tennis courts, and a new 100x200-foot dressage arena will finish the expansion.

"We feel that dealing with these horses develops self-confidence," Davis says. "If anybody tried to get on a horse who doesn't know what they're doing, that horse is going to take them for a ride. You can't fake it with a horse."

"We've had a few experiences," Ed Davis explained, "where people have come in with wonderful horses they wanted to give Culver. But they see those standing stalls and it just turns them off. We anticipate that with these new facilities and the brighter, better caring areas for the animals that we'll be able to receive real quality donations. Better horses and that second arena will allow our riders opportunities to polish up their skills so they'll do better in the competitions."

Ed's preferred form of competition is polo. Born and raised on a ranch in Midland, Texas, he disliked ranching but loved horses. At a military high school in New Mexico, he learned polo and went on from 1973 until 1990 to play professionally and to breed and train polo ponies. He returned to school to get a teaching credential. In 1990, Culver called him, looking for a polo coach, and five years after he arrived he moved into the role of horsemanship director. As an experienced horseman and a trained educator, it was a good match.

"We feel that dealing with these horses develops self-confidence," he said. "If anybody tried to get on a horse who doesn't know what they're doing, that horse is going to take them for a ride. You can't fake it with a horse. We truly believe that we have one of the best leadership programs at this school right here in our horsemanship department."

Grand Central Farm
Brewster, New York

The Ultimate Barn in Innovation and Elegance

"I was one of those little horse-crazy kids," Robin Greenwood explained, "and my mother was horse-crazy. In fact, the first riding I did was when we took lessons together when I was really little, my mother, my older brother, me, and my little brother. We used to go trail riding together."

In the decades that followed, Robin graduated from novice to accomplished rider, from amateur competitor and champion to professional champion, teacher, trainer, and breeder. As a horse-crazy teenager, she rode with Ronnie Mutch in Weston, Connecticut, at Nimrod Farm. Nimrod was a four-hour drive from her home and what started out as a Friday evening through Sunday session became a regimen of cut classes. In her junior year of high school, she missed 80 of 180 class days, driving down on Friday morning and back home Monday night. Yet, compelled as she was as a rider, she also made National Honor Society with straight As. It was at Mutch's stables that she and her mother acquired the first of Robin's great horses, Grand Central, a thoroughbred off the race track, in 1973.

"He had been champion at some really big shows," she said, "but no one thought that necessarily was going to happen every week. Then, literally from the time we bought him, he was champion at every show with Ronnie riding him." Robin showed him in amateur classes. Through 1974, Robin and Grand Central won amateur hunter champion at the Devon Horse show and he was champion of the working hunters at the Cape Cod show with Ronnie. But on the way home from Cape Cod, Grand Central collicked and died. "It was an incredibly major blow," Robin recalled.

"For me to breed ponies would be heaven," Robin Greenwood said about her farm. "For Paul, building something is what he does.... This was the perfect project."

One of architect Jeff Pearson's challenges was to diminish the scale of the enclosed arena behind the barn. Pearson suggested lowering the grade by 12 feet, which also benefited the perspective from the lower outside arena behind the barn.

A few weeks later Robin and her mother had a new horse, one they named Twentieth Century Limited because, as her mother explained, it was the finest train in and out of Grand Central station.

"He was the horse of a lifetime," Robin said. "He tried so hard, and he was so kind. He did a lot of things well. He wasn't big or beautiful, but this horse was maybe the best mover of his time, again a thoroughbred. In 1976, he was the American Horse Show Association Amateur Hunter Owner national champion." Robin's horse business had become rather large. She and her mother had three other horses so they established themselves as a Chapter S corporation, Grand Central Incorporated.

Robin leased a barn, competed with her own horses, and occasionally hired professionals to help her at horse shows. She turned professional in 1978 and began teaching. In 1985 she started Grand Central Show Stables, teaching and showing

horses until 1996. Those last few years, she rode less often in shows and more at the farm on kids' horses. "I have always loved ponies my whole life.

"I was very good at teaching kids to ride ponies, which is a really interesting thing," she said. "It doesn't sound like it, but in the horse show business there are a lot of people good at it. But most of the people who teach children to ride ponies have as their goal to get the kids started on horses. I got them on ponies because I wanted them to be on ponies. I became a specialist at it. I had quite a few successful clients. The kids were champion at Devon, Harrisburg, Washington, at the Meadowlands, at the Pony Finals. I loved it. I completely loved it."

Still, she retired in 1996. She and her husband, Paul, had adopted their first child the previous fall. Paul Greenwood owned Old Salem Farm, which he had built into a prestigious show site farm. But his involvement at Old Salem had evolved

Exterior stall doors provide ventilation and light, as well as additional egress in an emergency. Sliding stall doors inside the exterior walls restrain and protect the horses when the outer doors are open. The 20-stall barn is based on Kentucky thoroughbred barn layouts.

Jeff Pearson was concerned that horses coming upon one another from one aisle to another would get startled. He solved the problem by shaving corners off the tack room on the left and the wash stalls on the right.

into his being the man who answered questions from people running the farm for him. They undertook construction of a large house, a project that took four years. Robin recalled, "People would say to me, 'Oh yeah, builders, I know what that's like!' I told them, 'No, there's no problem with the builder here. Not at all.'" That got them thinking.

"For me to breed ponies would be heaven. For Paul, building something is what he does. He has such a sense of design and space and vision about things. Paul is best at the details. This was the perfect project." Paul had been a rider, involved both with the American Horse Show Association and the United States Equestrian Team. Building a farm for Robin to breed and train ponies was an opportunity for them to work on something together. They bought a 300-acre retired cattle ranch outside Brewster, New York, in 2002. They contacted Roger Allman of Farm Clinic in Lexington, Kentucky, to help them. Allman is a soils and grass expert who advises dozens of thoroughbred farms on the proper mix of grasses for horse pastures and turnouts. After visiting their property, he invited them to visit Lexington to get ideas for their farm and barn.

"Before we left, Paul asked me if I knew what I wanted for a barn," Robin recalled. "I knew exactly. There was only one kind for me. Everybody and their mother wants courtyards and they want this and that. I knew we were going to have a 20-stall

"The Greenwoods wanted something not only functional, but also that would have a strong architectural character to it," Jeff Pearson explained, "and that would have a sensitive warmth to it. That led us to consider wood."

barn. I wanted to be able to walk out of my office, look left and right, and see what people are doing and what's going on.

"So I drew it. Here's where the office goes. Here's where the tack room goes, here are the wash stalls. I gave the paper to Paul and we got down to Lexington . . . and that's what they all are. That's a Kentucky barn!" On one of their stops, they saw Overbook Farm.

"There we thought, 'Okay, we'll just stay here. We'll just buy this farm and forget about everything else.' Roger told us about Jeff Pearson, the architect in Versailles, who had designed it." Pearson came up to New York and walked as much of the overgrown ranch as possible with Paul and Robin and their house builder, Tim Taylor.

"We started pretty much from scratch with that blank slate of land," Pearson recalled. "They liked the style of the horse farms of Kentucky and they wanted something of that flavor. We designed the paddocks, road layouts, how utilities were to go, where fences would go. They had an approach that's different from Kentucky farms with a series of large run-in

sheds for many of their horses to get out of the weather, and get feed and water without needing additional barns. Then we'd just build one barn which really is there for breeding and foaling operations, and for some of the special horses that are in training or might be in line for sale.

"Much of the scale we derived for Grand Central came from the buildings at Overbrook and those came from old Kentucky tobacco barns. In the Kentucky vernacular of barn structures the tobacco barn is a big tall space where you can hang a lot of tobacco up high. You paint the building black so it heats up to dry and cure the leaves more easily. You put a vent at the ridge to let out the hot air and help air flow across the tobacco to dry it properly, to not stay moist or damp which causes mold."

Sidewall height in Kentucky and at Grand Central, and the large volume within the upper area of the barn, partially were aesthetic considerations. But Jeff, Paul, and Robin understood that good ridge ventilation promotes significantly better air quality within the barn. Paul researched doors, stall equipment,

The arena measures 108 feet wide by 180 feet long and reaches about 45 feet to the peak of the clerestory. Steel trusses would have worked, but the Greenwoods preferred the warmth of wood, so glue-laminated wood trusses filled the assignment.

Grand Central Trainer Siobhan Latchford works with Devilmint, a thoroughbred/Welsh pony cross, in the arena. While the barn and arena are unheated, a large lounge (behind the bay window) allows visitors to watch trials, workouts, and shows from somewhat warmer comfort.

and all the other hardware and equipment in detail, making his recommendations to Jeff as they went. Stall doors open to the floor, and wide-open stall fronts allow cross breezes to enter low and exit through the roof.

"The Greenwoods wanted something not only functional but also that would have a strong architectural character to it, and would have a sensitive warmth to it. That led us to consider wood." The desire for a clean barn and a barn easy to clean led to the decision to keep spans open using glue-laminated wood trusses for ceiling and roof supports. A false ceiling hid conduit and other barn structure that attracted dust, cobwebs, and birds. It also provided a smooth surface for an innovative double-rising smoke and heat detector system connected to an elaborate on-site fire suppression system.

"Paul worked with Tim and me on specific details down to door trims, moldings, and the sizes of mullions on the windows, sizes and proportions for doors and windows," Jeff recalled. "How we formulated the cupola, how we did all the elements that were the tactile details for the building . . . . Paul has a very strong interest in that."

Jeff collaborated with Lucas Equine Equipment who helped design stall fronts, doors, grillwork, and hardware that fit the elegant arched stalls under an architectural crown molding. This housed center-aisle and inside-stall lighting.

One major consideration was size. The Greenwoods wanted the barn far enough from the road so its mass would not intrude on the area, yet near enough to provide easy access. Jeff designed a roadway approach that swung north and crested a slight hill before looping toward the barn a short way down the hill. The land at that point fell away naturally to a large pond. The scale of the arena could have overpowered the elegant barn. Jeff solved that challenge by moving the barn nearer the road but carved into the hillside and he sliced away more of the lower hillside to accommodate the 108x180-foot arena.

Jeff Pearson, like many of his contemporaries, cites Frank Lloyd Wright when asked about architects he admires or whose work inspires him. This barn utilizes a Wright technique of dramatic transition. Leaving the barn for the attached arena leads through a long descending enclosed corridor. Its constant horizontal roof height creates a subtle funnel effect but it gives little hint to the scale of the arena ahead. Returning from the covered ring through the connector to the barn reverses the effect and the uphill climb prepares horses and riders for the more intimate proportions of the handsome barn.

"The covered show ring," Pearson explained, "forced us to look at several options for dimensions and sizes. We built the hipped roof on the arena with a raised clerestory to allow ventilation and light, and to give the building proportional

In order to hide plumbing and electric conduit, Jeff Pearson and builder Tim Taylor fitted false ceilings. The open wedges shroud a double-rising heat and smoke detector system where, if smoke slips past the lower detector, the upper catches it. Paving bricks set on their side form the floor of the central entry.

Initially, the covered show ring was to be a separate structure attached only by a covered breezeway. Over time, Pearson and the Greenwoods concluded that integrating the two buildings together might be a means to making the two scales work together even though they are vastly different.

height while minimizing the scale enough so that it would not dominate the barn." Glue-laminated wood trusses support this soaring roofline. While the arena is 15 feet taller than the barn, its placement a dozen feet below the barn and 80 feet behind it brings it into visual proportion. Much of the success of the two buildings Jeff credits to builder Tim Taylor, a craftsman he describes as "a furniture maker who builds buildings."

Robin makes it clear that horses bring a sense of reality to her life, keeping, as she says, "everything in perspective. You're caring for other living things that have personalities and quirks that are all unusual as your own children's might be. They are dependent on you and you are responsible for them.

"My fascination with ponies boils down to memories: I can picture myself year-in and year-out standing at the end gate at Madison Square Garden, talking to a 10-year-old about the course they're about to walk through the gate and go jump. And I look at their pony and think, 'Why would that animal walk into this ring, with all the lights and the crowd and the strange jumps, and pick up a canter at one end and make a circle and jump a course and stop when they're asked? They do this out of the goodness of their being. Out of enjoying their interaction with someone they trust.

"In this day and age, there are a lot of people who have gotten away from real life, and they're dedicated to their own importance and the things their importance can bring them. So many people that I know have tried to build beautiful barns—and everybody should have the barn they want. But for me, to see these barns, so often these structures are built to be a work of art more than a working barn. And I have the working barn that's the work of art."

Each of the 20 stalls backs up ceiling fire detectors with infrared and ultraviolet sensors, as well as closed-circuit cameras, coupled to a 600-gallon-per-minute fire suppression system fed by a pond on the farm. Each stall has an outside hinged and inside sliding door to aid in evacuating animals.

"Most people who teach children to ride ponies have as their goal to get the kids started on horses," Robin Greenwood said. She got them on ponies because she wanted them riding ponies. "I loved it. I completely loved it."

Lucky Dog Ranch
Somis, California

Winning over the Owner
with Bold New Ideas and Design Awards

"It's interesting, the evolution of this barn," Steve Sharpe said. "My friend and architect, Zoltan Pali, and I have been working on this project for many years. I bought this property, 40 acres, back in 1988. I was going to have him design a house and plan the land. We had all these ideas about how to shape this barn. I wanted to have an old-fashioned red barn that was an out-in-the-field-type barn."

But old-fashioned is not what Pali does.

"Depending on the mood I'm in . . ." Pali laughed. "Would I say I'm a hard-assed modernist? I have before but it would be hard for me to put a style label on my work. We try to boil things down to their essence, to capture the particular situation in that particular time and place that we are in, to solve the problem in an elegant and artful way."

Pali had met Sharpe in 1987. Sharpe is a commercial drywall contractor. His company finishes hotels, medical centers, shopping malls, and airport control towers, rather than individual homes. But he had a friend who needed a room addition and Pali was working late one day at his job with Solberg & Lowe in Santa Monica. The client was pleased with the result, and when Steve needed to do his own office in a new building, he went to Solberg & Lowe but asked for Pali. Their friendship grew from there.

"At the time he bought this piece of property," Zoltan recalled, "he was going to build a house there and he wanted me to draw it up for him. He showed me a picture and it was a Georgian-style home." He started to laugh again. "I said, 'Well, Steve, I'd like to do the project, but I don't know if I can do that . . . .'"

When owner Steve Sharpe first talked to friend and architect Zoltan Pali about a barn for his new ranch home, Sharpe had in mind an old-fashioned little red barn in a field. What he got instead was a radical concept that won American Institute of Architects (AIA) design awards.

As owner Steve Sharpe says, every barn needs a swing, and this rope is his. In the background, dawn breaks across the stalls of his compact innovative barn.

It is geometric simplicity. The barn is based on 12-foot square grids and provides four stalls for what the horse-hobbyist owner calls his "pretty, giddy-up horses." These are "manageable horses so if somebody wanted to come over and ride a horse, they don't have to be a highly skilled rider to not get killed," he explained.

"We went through a big learning curve together. Even the house he has now is not what I would design now. But that is almost a 10-year-old design. Oddly enough, we went on for years during the design process on the house. Every so often, we'd talk about the barn. First he told me he wanted to buy an old red barn off a New Hampshire farm and move it out and rebuild it. I thought, 'Oh, my God, well, if that's what you want, then I'll see if I can help you.' But maybe I can design something . . . ."

"He was thinking of all these different shapes for the barn," Steve said, continuing the story. "We had a big crescent plan at one time, which would have been a sensational barn. He had some other barn ideas that were Spanish. We went through a little bit of an evolution, a variety of styles and designs and ideas. But he always came back to this modern kind of thing."

Steve describes himself as "a horse hobbyist. We have giddy-up horses. There are people who really are horse people and that's all they do. If you're a horse person, that's all you *can* do because you have to pursue it with that kind of passion and dedication."

Zoltan designed a large guest wing on Steve's house. There is a lighted tennis court on the east edge of the property. Steve considers

"We used a twelve-by-twelve grid, which is a twelve-by-twelve stable size," architect Zoltan Pali explained. "Everything we needed was worked out into that twelve-by-twelve steel structural system. The thing completely boils down to its essence as a structure."

The 12-foot wide main aisle opens onto a 24x24-foot atrium for tacking up horses or for sitting with wine and cigars after a leisurely ride in Sharpe's arena or over the trails nearby. The original concept called for eight stalls, but Sharpe changed the focus of the ranch from riding to weekend client entertainment.

it a place for him and his wife and their children to entertain their friends and his clients. In a business with pricing questions and scheduling challenges, he feels that the better he knows his clients, the easier it is to mitigate those problems if they occur. They concluded that if they were using their house in a "working way," they needed to have manageable horses, "so if somebody wanted to come over and get in the arena and ride a horse, they don't have to be a highly skilled rider to not get killed.

"If you've got good horses, you can't just put anybody on them. The better the horse, the better the rider has to be to control it.

"I was thinking of bringing a horse trainer in. When you have a lot of horses, you need to have a trainer there, unless you are a horse trainer. Lots of people do that, and if that's their passion, that's great. But we still were trying to invent what this barn was going to be."

Zoltan made countless sketches, likening the progress of his work to an old story about an artist commissioned to paint a rooster. The buyer agreed on the price and the artist told him to return in three weeks. When the time passed, the buyer returned but the artist said he had not completed it. Then he quickly sketched, drew in, and painted the rooster. The buyer

As Pali considered what to do with Sharpe's hay, he made countless sketches sacrificing one interior portion of the structure or another. The idea came to him on a Lifecycle one morning in the gym: With enough roof overhang, the hay would age and dry naturally as the outside wall covering. The appearance of the exterior would evolve day by day.

Steve Sharpe feeds his horses in the cool blue predawn. His barn and his home further up the driveway glow. Sharpe calls himself the "lucky dog" of the farm's name.

Castlebrook Barns, a Southern California barn builder, did the engineering work and construction from Pali's designs. Eventually, these called for a large, airy breezeway and abundant storage. The building measures 24x120 feet.

was outraged, feeling his price was far too high for just a few moments of work. The artist motioned to him to follow him to his studio. He opened the door to reveal hundreds of sketches, drawings, and studies of various roosters taped all over the walls. The buyer who thought he had received something hurried and abruptly conceived learned it was the result of many hours of contemplation and experimentation.

Zoltan and Steve settled on a shape for the barn so Steve could create the site pad and grade the property to begin construction of the house. Zoltan was working on the house design in 1998 and he thought he would submit it to a design contest sponsored by *Progressive Architecture Magazine*. He had gone to the gym early one morning and was pedaling away on the Lifecycle when his idea for the barn and its unusual hay storage concept came clear in his mind. He hurried into the office where he sketched it up. When he showed it to his colleagues, they agreed to enter it separately from the house. It was three days before the deadline and they didn't tell Steve. "I just thought, I'll do it." Pali recalled. "If it wins, it wins, and then I'll get him to build it." Building it was a condition of receiving the award.

"And lo and behold, it actually won!" he said. "I put Steve down as the owner. They called him up to verify that we had a contract and that it was a real project. He called me back, stunned.

"We used a 12-by-12 grid which is a 12-by-12 stable size. Everything we needed was worked out into that 12-by-12 steel structural system. And then it was just sort of an idea to deal with that particular material, the hay. What to do with it? Where are you going to put it? So that brought up the simple idea of the shelf and stacking the hay on the side of the

The 24x36-foot space originally conceived for a tractor and other lawn and garden equipment instead contains a Ping-Pong table, large-screen television, and a pool table. The social function of a horse barn for its human users is very important.

building. The thing completely boils down to its essence as a structure," Pali explained.

Because they now needed to build it, Steve and Zoltan firmed up plans. Castlebrook Barns took on the assignment, doing the engineering work as well on Zoltan's designs. Eventually these called for a large, airy breezeway and abundant storage. The building measures 24x120 feet. The 24x36-foot space originally conceived for a tractor and other lawn and garden equipment contains a ping-pong table, large-screen television, and a pool table. As other equestrian architects have recognized, the social function of the horse barn for its human users is very important.

"Zoltan made the aisles very wide to accommodate people because there is nothing like sitting around after a ride, having a glass of wine and a cigar, and talking to your friends. Originally the barn was going to be double stalls and have a bunch of horses in it. Then during this process, I decided to have fewer horses so this barn has taken on a role more like a party pavilion."

Zoltan joined Steve to complete the project and install 230 bales of hay along three sides. Many viewers are transfixed by the clearly visible structure of the building. When the jurors from the American Institute of Architects came to examine the structure before awarding its more recent citation, one of them laughed and said, "Ohh, this is a structure that you can eat."

Zoltan was pleased that "the project also had the Japanese notion of *wabi-sabi*, where you take elements and boil them

down to their essence," he said. One cultural historian, Richard Powell, defines the term as "nothing lasts, nothing is finished, nothing is permanent." Its inhabitants consuming a bale of hay a day, seven days a week, alters the façade over time.

Steve, who calls himself the "Lucky Dog" of the ranch name, did not get his red New Hampshire barn. Nor did he get a Georgian mansion from Pali. "You know," he said, "when you're working with an architect they're always breaking your heart because you are working through a process." As a popular music enthusiast with tunes from the 1940s, 1950s, and 1960s playing throughout the barn, he likened the experience to another piece of recent music that concluded you might not always get what you want but you will get what you need. He loves his barn and it thrills him to hear friends and visitors pronounce it gorgeous.

Steve's architect laughs again when he hears his client speak of a broken heart. "We came along together," Zoltan said, "and he came along a long way to where he is now. He's a completely different person in the way he sees architecture and design. Partially this is a result of working with me, and consequently my working with him . . ., I don't know if it has influenced me, but it has tested me and taken me in many different directions.

"I'm not trying to reinvent architecture every Monday morning. It's not about trying to create the next new thing. It's about trying to build a better building. To do a better job with what's around you."

Sharpe can close massive doors to shut up the barn on colder nights. Two doors fold back against the long front inside wall, while the others slide along the ends of the stalls. As Pali says, "It's not about trying to create the next new thing. It's about trying to build a better building."

Visitors often are fascinated by the building's clearly visible structure. When jurors from the American Institute of Architects came to examine the barn before awarding its more recent citation, one of them laughed and said, "Ohh, this is a structure that you can eat."

Meadow Farm
Santa Barbara, California

The Ultimate California Jewel

"My dream as a child was to have my horses where I live," Beth Gabler recalled with a smile. She had gotten her first horse when she was 11, but she used to pretend that her parents' garage was a barn.

"My mom's best friend had a thoroughbred farm on the shores of Chesapeake Bay in Maryland. We would go visit them. Walking into that barn, seeing the horses stick their heads out to see who was there, that was like being in heaven," she said. "The whole time we stayed at their house, I never left the barn. There was the bay with the sailboats. No! I was in the barn. I couldn't imagine having a place where you could walk in and horses would bring their heads out of the stalls to see you. It was a fantasy."

Beth's fantasy began early. She admits she was addicted to horses by age five. She and her best friend rode a tandem bike to the stables every day after school to take lessons. "That was as close as we could get to a farm where I grew up in Long Beach, California.

"When Lee and I got married, we moved to Malibu which is much closer to where the horses are and I started riding again. And this place certainly will help that go forward."

"This place" is a 14-acre parcel called Meadow Farm in Santa Barbara's Hope Ranch, a community within the city that is a horse-lover's paradise founded by horse lovers more than a century ago. A rough guess would estimate that 1 house in 10 in Hope Ranch has a stable. The community boasts 27 miles of riding trails. Two Mexican land grants totaling 6,460 acres formed the lands that now include the ranch. The recipient, Narisco Fabrigat, sold out to a sea captain, Tom Robbins, in 1846, whose widow sold it to a wealthy sheep rancher, Thomas W. Hope, and his wife, Delia,

Beth Gabler's strong desire to have her horses at home combined with her husband Lee's love of New England classic architecture to produce this eight-stall jewel. With the help of architect Mark Appleton, both of their dreams were fulfilled.

Farm Manager José Yanez grooms Sound Advice while barn manager and trainer Thea Sprecher checks leg wraps. Owners Lee and Beth Gabler designed the barn together after visiting other structures and poring over magazines and books.

in 1861. The Hopes built a large home and a flat race track for trotting horses. This may have initiated the equestrian interest that remains within the ranch to this day.

Over the next 50 years, the Southern Pacific Railroad cut across and then relocated just outside of Hope Ranch and hotel developers tried to make the area an upscale resort before wealthy families from Los Angeles started buying land and building elegant homes. They established polo grounds, hosted hunts and steeplechase events, and laid out the extensive bridle trails. Today Hope Ranch encompasses 1,850 acres. Meadow

Farm was established as early as the 1920s as a thoroughbred training farm. Its own flat track is still a part of the modern day property. It was the nucleus of this old farm that Lee and Beth Gabler acquired in 1996.

"We bought the property," Lee explained, "because we both really have a lot of good feelings about Santa Barbara. Beth went to school here, then spent another year living and working up here. She has lots of good friends here that matter to her. We were looking for a place to settle." They were adamant about putting some distance between them and Los

Angeles, where both of them have highly influential careers in the entertainment industry.

"I love architecture," Lee continued and started to laugh. "And when Beth conned me into buying this property 10 years ago because of her intense interest in horses . . ."

"And our growing herd . . .," she interjected.

". . . And we were planning to have a child," Lee added. "I knew if it were a girl, I was a lost cause in terms of horses." Their child is a daughter, now three, whom Beth already has had on horseback. Lee has lost to the horses, but he's found a way to exercise the passion of his life.

"I walk into houses and where most people look at the art on the wall or the fabric on a sofa, I look at the craftsmanship in terms of the woodworking, the tile work. It always has fascinated me, even as a child. We knew we were going to build a barn and then a house. I already had an idea.

"We wanted a traditional Eastern style that called for a really steep roof, something that was going to be an 8-in-12 pitch or even 11-in-12 [rising 8 or 11 feet in 12 feet of horizontal travel]. We knew that building the house we wanted would take years trying to get roof height variances. While we were anticipating the challenges that plan might entail, we decided—mainly

Thea Sprecher hugs Heartbre[...] in the courtyard between the b[...] and the similarly styled mainte[...] building in the background. Th[...] barn plan utilizes a cross-aisle[...] configuration with six stalls on[...] side, double wash-and-tack sto[...] two more box stalls, a laundry[...] room, storage closet, and a tro[...] room/lounge on the other.

Dusk at Christmastime highlights the shape of the barn, its roof, and its dormers, as well as the season's cheer from decorative lights. "Beth has a sentimental heart," Lee added, "and it is her love of her horses that created this barn."

because Beth has horses now and we were coming up here every weekend—to build the barn first. Also, it gave us an opportunity to get familiar with and get used to the local contractors before taking on the larger ordeal of building a new house."

Lee was born in New York, and though he has been on the West Coast since 1970, his love of New England classic architectural forms never has left him. As he and Beth conceived the barn and matching maintenance shed across the courtyard, certain elements were mandatory.

"The style of these two buildings," Lee explained, "the cupolas, the dormer windows, the entire layout of the barn, was ours." They found a willing architect to translate their

preferences into something readily buildable. Better than that, their architect, Mark Appleton, while very popular in the entertainment community in Los Angeles, grew up in Hope Ranch. Even more encouraging was Appleton's announced plans to establish offices in Santa Barbara. He assigned his associate, Eric Meyerowitz, to work with the Gablers, and Meyerowitz, while not a barn designer by trade, helped them with the details. "We gave him the layout of this place, told him we wanted open beams, tongue-in-groove walls."

Lee and Beth already had designed the barn together. They pored over magazines and went through books. Lee took a trip through Virginia, and Beth spent four months living in England

Stall doors and hardware came from Lodden of England. Closed-circuit television cameras monitor each of the 12x12-foot stalls, as well as the aisles and exterior entries.

"We didn't want a barn that was just functional and industrial looking," Lee explained. "We wanted a barn that you would walk into and, if you know horses, you would know they were well cared for; that it would be more than adequate for the animals we were caring for."

Lodden's stall hardware gave the Gablers the look and feel of classic New England equestrian facilities they desired. Architect Mark Appleton and associate Eric Meyerowitz took the Gabler's request for open beams and tongue-in-groove wallboards and integrated structure with style.

Thea Sprecher adjusts the bridle on Heartbreaker before an exercise ride, while Jose Yanez grooms Sound Advice before turnout. The two wide wash-and-tacking stalls with doors to the outside provide Sprecher or Yanez or owner Beth Gabler plenty of room to work without interfering with one another.

At the end of the day, a stable hand leads horses down from the pastures. The 14-acre property came with a flat training track, which the Gablers slightly modified and retained as an exercise ring.

working on a project and visiting horse farms whenever she could. Both of them were very familiar with the English stalls supplier Loddon, and knew this manufacturer had the look and quality they sought. They spent a weekend together with friends touring barns and stables throughout the San Diego area.

"All the barns we saw were very functional," Lee explained. "I don't want to say 'industrial,' but they were functional. They didn't have the charm we were looking for. We didn't want a barn that was just functional and industrial-looking. We wanted a barn that you would walk into and, if you know horses, you would know they were well cared for; that it would be more than adequate for the animals we were caring for. At the same time, you would feel the same way you felt walking into your house. That's the reason we went into the detail that we did.

"It's really a labor of love. We can walk through this barn at any time, Beth and I, and we're able to take a great deal of pride and enjoyment out of just looking at the way things are put together and built here. I'm a fanatic about the details," Lee admitted. "This is more than just a place to hang the hat. It's an extension of our personalities and our environment."

The barn plan utilizes a crossed aisle configuration. Two wide wash stalls with doors to the outside leave Beth or her trainer and barn manager, Thea Sprecher, and the ranch manager, Jose Yanez, plenty of room to groom, tack, and saddle animals without interfering with one another. It almost was a textbook perfect project. The architectural review committee in Hope Ranch vetoed their plans for a 10-stall barn as too large for the property. So Meyerowitz, Appleton, and the Gablers shrunk

The trophy room gives the feel of an intimate sitting room. "I'm a fanatic about the details," Lee Gabler admitted. "This is more than just a place to hang the hat. It's an extension of our personalities and our environment."

"It's a big thing to have horses where you live," Beth Gabler said. "And we're very fortunate to have this place. Our horses have a comfortable, safe, healthful barn that we love to be in, too.... It's a great fantasy to be able to have the horses here, right here, this close."

the barn, decreasing not only stalls but also storage space, as well as the original dimensions of their tack room and trophy room on the north end of the barn. Presently five of their horses live in the barn. They will bring another two from a boarding stable in Malibu, and add a pony for their daughter. Beth has two thoroughbreds, two Dutch warmbloods, and an Appendix quarter horse. They contracted the original flat track slightly and widened it to enhance drainage. It surrounds four spacious meadow-like pastures and these surround an outdoor ring.

"My horses are like my favorite people to me," Beth explained. "Every one of them has a personality."

"Put it this way," Lee interrupted. "If I come home and say 'I'm not feeling well, I'm going to bed,' and at the same time the vet says Sounder, one of Beth's horses, is not feeling well, Beth will say, 'Lee, go lie down,' and then she'll run to the barn."

"It's a big thing to have horses where you live," Beth said. "And we're very fortunate to have this place. Our horses have a comfortable, safe, healthful barn that we love to be in, too. Lee has a very fulfilling job, but he is a woodworker at heart and his passion is in the details."

"And Beth has a sentimental heart," Lee added, "and it is her love of her horses that created this barn."

"It's a great fantasy," Beth concluded, "to be able to have the horses here, right here, this close."

Acknowledgments

First and foremost, my thanks go to friend and Photoshop mentor Rich Reid of Ojai, California. Forty years of shooting transparencies and developing some skill at it has made learning the new trick of high-quality digital image processing seem like rocket science. Rich was the scientist who got the rocket off the ground and into orbit.

Producing this book required the cooperation and encouragement of many people across North America. In particular, I am grateful to: John Asher, vice president of racing communications, Churchill Downs, Louisville, Kentucky; Samantha Barber, stables manager, Fork Stables, Norwood, North Carolina; John Blackburn, architect, Blackburn Architects, P.C., Washington, D.C.; Peter Block, architect, Peter Block Architects, Atlanta, Georgia; Bettina Chandler, Ojai, California; Jamie Charron, horse specialist, University of Vermont Morgan Horse Farm, Weybridge, Vermont; Glyn Clarke, International Equestrian Design, IED Sopra, Montreal, Quebec, Canada; Jim Cogdell, Cogdell Spencer Advisers, Charlotte, North Carolina; Donald and Karen Cohn, Ballena Vista Farms, Ramona, California; Tom Croce, architect, Thomas L. Croce Architects, Lebanon, Ohio; Steve Davis, director of farm, University of Vermont Morgan Horse Farm, Weybridge, Vermont; Jennifer Donovan, Equestrian Services, LLC, Annapolis, Maryland; Julie Eldridge Edwards, curator of collections, Shelburne Farms, Shelburne, Vermont; Elric Endersby, New Jersey Barn Company, Princeton, New Jersey; Bob Evans, Tenlane Farm, Versailles, Kentucky; Tom Evans, Tenlane Farm, Versailles, Kentucky; Joe Fargis, Stoneleigh Farm, Middleburg, Virginia; Marilyn Fisher, Reagan Ranch, Goleta, California; Eric Flemming, Hardwick, Massachusetts; Genevieve Frost, Vienna, Virginia; Elizabeth and Lee Gabler, Meadow Farms, Santa Barbara, California; Cheryl Garrido, stable manager and trainer, Chesapeake Dressage Institute, Annapolis, Maryland; Martin and Jane Garrick, Solana Beach, California; Marcelino Gordillo, grounds manager, Ballena Vista Farms, Ramona, California; Robin and Paul Greenwood, Grand Central Farms, Brewster, New York; Berkeley Gunnell, Greyledge Stables, Upperville, Virginia; John Hall, Freedom Farm Equestrian Research Institute, Ravenna, Ohio; Herbie Hames, designer, Concord, North Carolina; Bonnie Jenkins, director of United States Equestrian Team Foundation, Hamilton Farm, Gladstone, New Jersey; Siobhan Latchford, barn manager, Grand Central Farm, Brewster, New York; Ed Little, director of equestrian education, Culver Academies, Culver, Indiana; Joe Martinolich, CMW architects, Lexington, Kentucky; Carey Miller, Caper Lea Stables, Trappe, Maryland; Manuel Ochoa, farm manager, Ballena Vista Farms, Ramona, California; Rick Ollett, chief administrative officer, Culver Academies, Culver, Indiana; Zoltan Pali, architect, SPF: Studio Pali Fekete Architects, Culver City, California; Jeff Pearson, architect, Pearson & Peters Architects, Lexington, Kentucky; Mason Phelps, Phelps Media Group, Wellington, Florida; Beth Pico, assistant farm manager, Ballena Vista Farms, Ramona, California; Vickie Rasmussen, office manager, Ballena Vista Farms, Ramona, California; Janet Richardson-Pearson, Chesapeake Dressage Institute, Annapolis, Maryland; Liz and Jerry Reilly, Hardwick, Massachusetts; William Rodgers, Freedom Farm Equestrian Research Institute, Ravenna, Ohio; Ben Rogers, general manager, Heronwood Farm, Upperville, Virginia; Janet and Ed Sands, Santa Barbara, California; Fred and Karen Schaufeld, New River Farm, Leesburg, Virginia; Lou Seiler, Casa Loma, Toronto, Ontario, Canada; Mary B. Schwab, Stoneleigh Farm, Middleburg, Virginia; Robert Smith, Heronwood Farm, Upperville, Virginia; Rosalyn and Dan Smythe, Round Lot Farm, Medfield, Massachusetts; Karen Snyder, manager, Fork Stables, Norwood, North Carolina; Thea Sprecher, barn manager, Meadow Farms, Santa Barbara, California; Hilary Sunderland, marketing and special events, Shelburne Farms, Shelburne, Vermont; Tim Taylor, construction manager, Grand Central Farm, Brewster, New York; Tony Terry, director of publicity, Churchill Downs, Louisville, Kentucky; Sarah Thomas, Biltmore Estate, Asheville, North Carolina; William Tobin, retired engineer, Townsend, Montana; Torrance Watkins, Hardwick, Massachusetts; Mark Wray, architect, Millcreek Post & Beam, Saluda, North Carolina; Dafna Zilafro, SPF Architects, Culver City, California; and Peter Zukoski, Caper Lea Stables, Trappe, Maryland.

In addition, I want to thank Donna Griffith of Donna Griffith Photography, Toronto, Ontario, Canada, for access to and permission to use her wonderful images of Casa Loma stables. I also am grateful to Marshall Webb of Shelburne, Vermont, for access to and permission to use his beautiful images of the horse breeding barn and the carriage barn at Shelburne Farms in Shelburne, Vermont. Both of these fine photographers add much to this book.

I am most grateful to my editor, Amy Glaser, for offering me this great project, and to my publishers Michael Dregni at Voyageur Press, and Zack Miller at MBI Publishing, for their encouragement and willingness to juggle schedules to allow me produce this book.

Finally, I thank my partner in life, Carolyn Chandler Leffingwell, for her encouragement, support, and hard work with me on this book. Our first date many years ago was a several-hour-long horseback ride. To share our love of horses and our admiration for great architecture on this project was a glorious gift.

To all of you who love your horses and aspire to give them a great barn home, I hope you enjoy this book,

Randy Leffingwell
—Santa Barbara, California

Index